A WORLD ELSEWHERE

A WORLD ELSEWHERE

The Autobiography of Sir Michael Hordern
with Patricia England

MICHAEL O'MARA BOOKS LIMITED

This paperback edition published in 1994 by
Michael O'Mara Books Limited
9 Lion Yard, Tremadoc Road, London SW4 7NQ

Copyright © 1993 by Patricia England

First published in Great Britain in 1993

A CIP catalogue record for this book is available from the
British Library

ISBN 1–85479–923–1

Designed by Mick Keates
Typeset by Florencetype Ltd, Kewstoke, Avon
Printed and bound in England by Cox and Wyman, Reading

There is a world elsewhere
  Coriolanus Act III Scene 3

For Patricia

CONTENTS

CHAPTER 1

Life at the Poplars

My grandfather Murray married on the rebound. He was assisting Brunel to build a branch line for the Great Western Railway, between Slough and Windsor, for the benefit of Queen Victoria, when he met and fell in love with Annie Tyrwhitt Drake, the daughter of a wealthy Buckinghamshire landowner. The Tyrwhitt Drakes owned most of south Buckinghamshire and were obviously people of considerable standing in the area and, thinking grandfather's career as assistant engineer to Isambard Kingdom Brunel insufficient qualification for a future son-in-law, smartly sent him on his way. Whereupon he upped and went to Ireland and married Fanny Brereton, the sad widow of an army officer killed in the Indian Mutiny. They settled in Bray, County Wicklow, and had a family of five sons and a daughter, Margaret Emily, who later became my mother.

Grandfather was obviously an imaginative man with plenty

of initiative although not much business sense. Turning his hand to pharmaceutical discovery, he invented Milk of Magnesia, which has been calming the world's stomachs ever since. This made him a good deal of money and when, after giving him six children, poor Fanny Brereton died, grandfather returned to Buckinghamshire, once more asking for the hand of his former love, Annie Tyrwhitt Drake. The reception he received was a good deal more friendly this time and he was welcomed into the family. He and his new wife returned to Bray, County Wicklow, to bring up the six motherless children.

The Milk of Magnesia business prospered and the family lived in some style, although they would have been a good deal richer if grandfather had not decided to patent the miraculous compound only in the British Empire and its colonies, ignoring the rest of the world. His astute secretary, Dinniford, to whom was left a good deal of the managing of the Magnesia business, rectified grandfather's mistake, making himself a very rich man at the same time. Eventually, Grandfather Murray was killed after a drunken hunting accident and his body brought home on a hurdle. Shortly afterwards, Grandmother Tyrwhitt swept the dust of Ireland from her feet and retired to Little Kimble in Buckinghamshire, taking Margaret Emily with her and eventually sending her to St Audries School for Girls, Somerset. She received a very good education and a lifelong love of literature, which was to prove a consolation years later when she found herself living an isolated and lonely life in a remote house on Dartmoor.

My father, Ned, came from a very different background. His father was a much-respected vicar of Holy Trinity Church, in Bury, Lancashire, noted for his holiness and 'remarkable power of training people in the life of devotion'. Ned also came from a large family of brothers and sisters and it was through one of his brothers that he first met my mother.

Margaret Emily had originally been engaged to one of Ned's

elder brothers and everything was arranged for them to be married. Then she met Ned. He was an attractive man and must have looked very dashing in his uniform of Lieutenant in the Royal Indian Marines. She fell in love with him and followed him out to Burma; they were married in Rangoon Cathedral on 28 November 1903. The *Church Times* carried this account of my mother's travels:

There may be many of her friends in Kimble who would like to hear of Miss Murray after she left England, November 4th 1903, to join the *Warwickshire* at Marseilles, carrying with her so many good wishes for her future happiness and also a most charming present of a silver sugar basin subscribed by almost everyone in the Parish.

She had a good voyage and was much interested in going through the Suez Canal, where the desert scenery reminded her of *The Bible* and the Arabs, in their long white burnouses and turbans, she said, looked like Moses and Abraham. The next stop was Colombo, Ceylon, where she and her friends went to an hotel on shore for three days. Men and women were all dressed alike—in white petticoats with high combs in their heads. Four days more brought her to Rangoon, Burma, where Mr Hordern and his brother met her on November 28th, and some friends drove her to the Cathedral and gave her away, and tea, cakes and champagne followed after the ceremony. A train journey of 18 hours took them to Mandalay, where she has a charming house high above the river, and the next week was occupied in settling and unpacking her presents, where we may leave her trying to make a native cook and a Burmese boy understand her.

Their first child, Geoffrey Edward, was born two years later in Akyab, in Burma. He was an enormous baby and was immediately christened 'Shrimp' by his doting parents, a name that he keeps to this day at the grand age of eighty-six. Two years later in Northchurch, Hertfordshire, my brother Peter appeared and, after a decent interval of four years, I made my début. By this time, my mother had moved back to England and I was born on 3 October 1911 at The Poplars, Berkhamsted, Hertfordshire. I don't remember much about The Poplars, although I have been back to see it and looked again at the room where I was born. I was pleased to see that the magnificent mulberry tree, which gave us such bumper harvests of delicious mulberries, was still there. It was a lovely tree for climbing and was a great feature of the garden with its big strong trunk and great branches, perfect for small boys. My brothers climbed like monkeys, leaving their wretched little brother standing below, longing to join in. They built a splendid platform high in the branches. It was all of eight or nine feet off the ground, but it seemed miles to me. We called it 'The Jolly Nest' after *Swiss Family Robinson*. My brothers fashioned a huge net out of string and heaved me, together with a picnic of sandwiches and milk, up into its mysterious branches. We kept quite an establishment at The Poplars. Those were the days when Ned was in full employment in the Indian Marines and so money was not the problem it was later to become. We could afford a cook, scullery maid, housekeeper, nanny, gardener and gardener's boy, as well as running a pony and trap. I loved the pony trap and would lisp that I would 'like to go and see taag' which, translated by the family, meant that I should enjoy going down to see the stags. This entailed a longish drive to Ashridge Park. Years later, after the war, it became a postgraduate establishment and I was invited to go down there to give a talk about 'the theatre'. Obviously, feeling I was a bit of an authority by that time, I accepted, giving a talk confidently entitled 'The Actor Today'. So I went down to 'see taag' again.

I remember more about the garden of The Poplars than about the house itself. We had the most wonderful fun in the garden. Simple pleasures: I remember the 'box on wheels'. A splendid box with wheels attached to a sort of chassis in which we would career down a convenient slope in the garden path, just right for a box on wheels. I noticed with dismay, when I recently revisited the garden, that the path had gone, so you couldn't get a box on wheels down there any more.

My first five years passed cheerfully, surrounded as I was by an adoring mother, brothers, Florrie my nanny, Cook and Dart. For some reason we found it impossible to get our infant tongues round the name Margaret and so she was always called Dart, and her older sister, who used to come and stay, was called 'the other Dart'. She was my father's younger sister and she lived with us a good deal. I was very fond of Dart, who fascinated me by making the most lovely lace on a huge cushion. I have no idea how she managed to live as she had no money and no job. I can only think her brothers must have rallied round to give her a small allowance. Anyway, she was a dear and we loved her.

I caught my first fish at Berkhamsted. I was about five and Shrimp had kindly taken me fishing for the first time. I can vividly remember it. The canal bank, a bunch of rushes on my right and casting out the float with a worm on a hook. Watching intently, then seeing the float quiver and dip and slide away and disappear. Shrimp shouting at me to strike and out came, oh joy, a little tiddler, a small roach about five inches long. I burst into tears at the excitement of it all. For years afterwards I cried whenever I caught a fish. There was something primeval about it, an event so earth-shattering that I just wept. I did cry fairly easily and I still do. My brothers disparagingly called me 'Streaks' because of the subtle combination of dirt and tears. I was not allowed to take the fish home to show Mummy as Shrimp had been told that you throw back fish which are under a certain length so, in order to show his superiority, he made me put it back, but from that moment I was, so to speak, hooked. All I wanted to do was to take it home and show Mummy. If I had been allowed to do that, I might have been cured. But as it was, I had to go back and catch another. And I have been going back ever since.

Fishing has been a lifelong passion with me. My devotion to it has caused huge problems in my personal life. My nearest and dearest have often felt unloved and neglected as I strode off for a glorious few days on the Wye or the Test. It is such a magnificent sport that, although I rather regret the pain caused by my obsession, once I am on the riverbank there is nowhere else I want to be.

In 1916, when I was five, my enchanted life at The Poplars went through a sea change. My mother decided to visit Father, who was in India. It was intended to be only a short visit, but war was raging round Europe and it became obvious that it was too dangerous to return, so she remained in India until 1918. I was sent to join my brothers at a prep school in Sussex called Windlesham. As I was so young, my nurse Frances was sent with me.

I suppose it sounds rather sad for such a small child to be separated from his mother, but I can't remember feeling any real unhappiness about it. Brothers Shrimp and Peter were already at the school and that, together with the comforting presence of nurse, took the edge off any pain I might have felt. In fact, the pain I do remember was more to do with the fact that I wasn't dressed in a nice uniform like the rest of the boys but had to wear a rather strange smock. No doubt it was a delightful and lovely garment but to me it was a silly girly smock.

As there were a few other tinies like me, they had a sort of kindergarten. We were the 'holiday boys' who, because of the war, were not able to join their parents, so stayed at school during the holidays. We had enormous fun being at school without schooling, with plenty of room to play. We had football, cricket pitches, trees to climb and swimming.

I was at Windlesham for nine years, which must be some kind of record. It was a wonderful school and still is. I am sure most of the reasons I settled in so well at such a tender age was due to the warmth and sensitivity of the headmistress, Mrs Charles Scott Malden, who had inherited the school after the sudden death of her husband in 1896.

Mrs Charles was a remarkable person. She was a short, comfortable woman who always wore black and overflowed the chairs. She was also inspiring, full of energy and ideas, running the school with great efficiency, helped by her three daughters, Euphemia, Marjory and Joyce, and her sister-in-law, Miss Rose, whom the boys christened 'Aunty Fusspot'. All Mrs Charles' energies were devoted to planning and organizing the school and raising the standard of education. It was a well-run place with big grounds and vegetable gardens. I remember the food being rather good except for something deeply unpleasant called 'coconut butter'. The rest of the country was enduring rationing and food shortages on account of the war but I think that on the whole we ate better than the boys who went home in the holidays and had to scrimp along on God knows what. We had the son of the local food administrator for Brighton and District at the school and I think quite a lot of undercover rations found their way to Windlesham. Even so, the food limitations that the 1914–18 war had imposed on the rest of the country certainly did affect us. The margarine was extended by mixing it with cornflour and I remember a rather strange bread made from a mixture of barley and oat flour and formed into balls the size of apples which we called 'elephant's eggs'. On the whole, the grub was plain and basic, but good.

When I was there the school was at Southern Cross, Portslade. But in 1935 it was moved to a beautiful Queen Anne house set high in the midst of the Sussex Downs. I revisited it a few months ago and it was fascinating to meet the present headmaster, who is the great great grandson of Mrs Charles.

My most successful activity at Windlesham was acting. I remember Asher 2. (They weren't much taken with Christian names at Windlesham; I was Hordern 3.) Asher 2 and I started a very specialist organization called the AAA. This stood for the classroom A Acting Association and we had a special rubber stamp to prove it. We tended to do everything by committee. We wrote, acted and directed, naturally giving ourselves the star parts. One of the plays, of which we were particularly fond, was an epic called *The Man with the Speckled Face*. Why the man had a speckled face I don't remember exactly, but I do remember enjoying the make-up very much and we were also very proud of the dramatic effect of torchlight through the bars of the prison, represented by a chair. We thought it very striking, but it was primitive compared to the magnificent production we staged out of doors in front of the rookery. This involved Julius Caesar, a Brontosaurus and some Druids. It had a complicated plot with some effective choral chanting of 'sinister dexter, sinister dexter' as the Roman Legions were heard approaching pursued by the Brontosaurus, represented by six small boys covered in rugs with a great mask head with properly moving parts, which I bravely killed in the last act. I always gave myself the best parts. After all, if you take the trouble to write the play . . . A boy called Waddy was the chief Druid. He must have liked the frock as he later became a bishop. A line that gave us particular pleasure was, in answer to the question 'Who drew this?', the stunning reply 'A Druid drew it Druid'. We thought this tremendously witty.

Most of the trees around the school were beech. These were very good to climb. Overlooking the cricket ground were three special beech trees known to us boys as the 'treble crossing'. As there were no low branches on the middle tree, you had to climb almost to the top of the first tree then swing across on a branch like a monkey. When you got to the top of the third tree this was known at the 'treble crossing'. This was the ultimate and only the most expert tree climbers could get to it. Heaven knows why we didn't get killed. We built a sort of platform hut at the top of the third tree from which we could watch the cricket, having risked our lives to get there.

Every moment of the day, from going to the loo after break-fast (this for some inexplicable reason was called 'lots') to last thing at night, when we were tucked up in the dorm, we were constantly on the go. There was great competition to be the first into the swimming bath each morning. The water in the swimming bath was almost never changed and became greener and greener. Why we didn't all get cholera I don't know. As soon as we heard the rising bell, we were off down the stairs and into the unheated water. Any boy who didn't find this absolutely delightful had to have a cold bath instead.

Altogether, my time at Windlesham was very happy. I was well liked and got on well with the Charles family, who were very fond of us Horderns. I was rather a pet. Perhaps too much so. In fact, I think I've been too much of a pet all my life.

As soon at the war was over in 1918, my father Ned, who was by now Port Officer in Calcutta, arranged for Mother to be shipped back to England, bringing with her our new little baby sister, Jocelyn, whom we immediately christened 'Doody'.

Doody happened in India. She was the daughter of a Mrs Reed, the wife of Colonel Reed, who was away fighting in the Gulf. Mother and father were taking a short leave in Dalhousie when mother was asked by a frantic local GP to assist him with Mrs Reed, who was about to give birth. With some trepidation, my mother helped to deliver a baby girl, and then another, and then another. These three infants were immediately christened, being named Violet, Pamela and

9

Jocelyn. The first baby, Violet, died almost immediately, followed shortly afterwards by the unfortunate Mrs Reed. As there didn't appear to be anyone to care for the children, Mother was left, literally, holding the babies. It was arranged that she should take the children back to England to be handed over into the care of their aunt, another Mrs Reed. The baby Pamela, who was brain-damaged, did not survive the journey and was buried at sea off the coast of Ceylon. Jocelyn was made of sterner stuff and thrived, arriving back in England with Mother, ready to be handed over to her aunt. However, there was much consternation in the families when it was discovered that the aunt was an agnostic. My mother was horrified, as was the child's grandmother, who pleaded with Mother to bring the child up as her own. Although doubting her ability to bring up a girl successfully, Mother had grown very fond of Jocelyn and agreed. So my brave parents adopted Doody. My father, Ned, was delighted. He adored her—she was the daughter he had always wanted—and we three boys were thrilled. Doody was completely absorbed into the Hordern family and my brothers were very much nicer to her than they were to me at that age.

When I was about eight, we left The Poplars and moved to Brighton. We stayed for a short time in two flats. The first was in Eton Square and the second was in Marine Parade, a lovely position overlooking the sea. We never really got into life in Brighton although I do remember fishing off the end of the Pier, sitting on a sort of grating and catching a rather large plaice. Most of the fish caught were of no great account so this caused a bit of excitement amongst the other fishermen. To my great delight and pride, the next time I went fishing I heard an old fisherman say to another, 'There's the boy who caught that big fish'.

About this time, Ned had retired from the Indian Marines with a pretty piddling pension which, I understand from my brother Shrimp, was about £40 a month. Such money as

10

the family had came from grandfather Murray's Milk of Magnesia mine. Hordern money was virtually non-existent. My parents bought a house in Haywards Heath and we embarked on 'family life' for the first time.

We bought a car, a 1905 Humber. We took a tent and always went westward for summer holidays. The first time in the new car, my parents, rather typically, went from cathedral to cathedral. On these expeditions, it was the height of the bell tower rather than the beauty of the architecture that impressed us children. It was an open car; the lid came down and we had two very long leather straps attached to the back. These were for Shrimp and Peter, who were travelling independently on bicycles, to hang on to when the going got tough. Imagine doing that nowadays. Anyway, off we chuffed—me, Ma, Doody, Ned driving and Peter and Shrimp hanging on behind.

My first moorland trout was caught on one of these family holidays, in about 1921, on our way in the family car to a summer holiday in Cornwall. Camping that night by the headwaters of the River Webbern, we successfully tickled trout, having no idea of the fishy delights that lay ahead of us three years later, when we were to live further downstream at Jordan, near Ponsworthy. Watching a float on canals and village ponds was one thing, but wild moorland trout were a thrilling new quarry, and wonderful eating.

We were absolutely devoted to our mother, Meg. She was not an emotional woman and we were not a very demonstrative family but she was very affectionate, particularly towards me. We were so devoted, so dependent upon her, that Ned was rather pushed onto the sidelines. We were never very close to him the way we were with Mummy. We were a card-playing family and he would play cards with us. We got on all right with him, but he was a remote man, a sort of interloper. He adored Doody and she was his Pet, but he never got on well with Peter. They really rubbed each other up the wrong way. The 'dislike',

11

if that's not too strong a word for it, was more on Peter's side. He was 'agin' Ned more than Ned was 'agin' Peter. In fact, Ned was very proud of Peter, who did very well at school and was a brilliant sportsman. Ned was not a clever man intellectually, although he was hard-working and had done pretty well in the service. But we didn't consult him. Peter was extremely intelligent, strong-minded and direct. He wasn't 'hidebound' like Ned. Later, when we moved to Dartmoor, there were terrible arguments, much shouting and slamming of doors, much driving away in the middle of the night.

I remember a terrible stand-up row between Peter and Ned about the pigeons. I can't remember the *casus belli* exactly but either Peter or Ned seemed to think that the pigeons were eating their young and must have their necks rung. The row grew to huge proportions, with Ned packing and saying he was going to leave this horrible family and take Doody with him, and me rushing out and pulling the plugs out of the car to prevent him. We were a very emotional family, great criers, although I never saw my mother the worse for tears.

I was fourteen when I left Windlesham. I hold the record for being the Windlesham boy who stayed the longest. I then joined my brothers at Brighton College. My brother Peter was an extremely popular chap, head of his house, in the first fifteen and a prefect. He later got a blue at Oxford and played rugby for England. A marvellous games player, he knew what balls did and they did what he told them to do. All this glory reflected upon me for a short time and gave me a certain amount of credibility until they found me out. I was no good at games at all. I didn't excel in any area except singing; I couldn't read music but I sang quite well.

Every Christmas we staged a production of a Savoy opera by Gilbert and Sullivan, and a great deal of time and trouble were expended upon it. My first part was the Duchess in *The Gondoliers*. I still remember quite a bit of it to this day and will burst into song at the slightest encouragement. For some reason, I could only sing falsetto by throwing my head back—I don't know why, perhaps because of the formation of my throat or vocal chords or something. This produces the strange effect of making me look like a chicken when I am singing. But in spite, or maybe because, of this, I was a great success as the Duchess and went on to play in the men's chorus in *Iolanthe*. The cast were all splendid upstanding chaps, and I was very small for my age and must have looked very funny, a tiny little chap right in the middle. I went on to sing in the men's chorus in *The Mikado* and finally the part of Major General in *The Pirates of Penzance*. Although I look back on this as being perhaps a start of the career that I finally embraced, I had absolutely no feeling that I was going that way at all. I had then no burning desire to become an actor.

We were not a theatre-going family at all. We went to the pantomime but never to plays. I didn't see a play till I was fifteen, when a friend of the family, a curate called Cyril Hudson (we were a great family for curates), took me during the holidays from Brighton to the Adelphi Theatre in London to see Jessie Matthews in *Evergreen*. You dressed up for the theatre in those days, and I wore a dinner-jacket for the first time. We grandly sat in the stalls. I absolutely adored it. Jessie Matthews was marvellous, all big, beautiful liquid eyes and a great pair of legs.

Cyril Hudson had been the curate at Berkhamsted and a great friend of my mother, who adored anyone in a dog collar. He rose in his profession to become Canon of St Albans. He was a great chap. Why he loved me I don't know but he was always treating me to this and that. He had married a very wealthy wife, who was also delightful, but they had no children, so perhaps I was the son he never had. He was good and kind and always coming up with helpful ideas like paying the school fees. He educated me more than either of my schools did and I still have books in my bookcase that he gave me. He was the only one to give me any theatrical encouragement.

When we moved as a family to Dartmoor, we didn't go near the theatre but we did have a wireless and a gramophone. I remember visiting a fellow Windlesham boy whose family had a five-valve wireless set, which in those days was something tremendously rich and glorious. It didn't have a loudspeaker (the headphones had to be passed round), but it was magic.

I was doing very well at Brighton College on what you might call the arts side but not so well on the sports side so, as it was a very keen shooting school, I opted for shooting. We won the Ashburton Shield, I remember, which was the highest honour a school could achieve in interschool shooting. Opting for shooting meant settling down at a shooting range with five rounds and shooting at a target. I was hopeless, missed it with all my rounds and thought, 'O Gawd, I shall have to play cricket', but I spotted a way out and that was to be a butt marker. This meant going down to the butts three days a week and marking the targets as they were hit. You had to turn a great target around quickly, put a patch where a bullet had gone, by which time someone was shooting at the next target on the other side, rather like a windmill, and then you slung it round again and up it went.

This operation allowed you not only to avoid the cricket but to smoke. So there we were having a lovely time, puffing away in the butts on the Sussex Downs. At least it got me off the cricket. I realize it must be a marvellous game and I can appreciate the love people have for it but it never captured me. Competitive games have never attracted me: too selfish, I suppose. I think of myself and don't think of the team. It is said that 'the game is more than the player of the game, and the ship is more than the crew'. Games should teach people team spirit and about working with other people. I never learnt that from sport although, in my own defence, I think I may say I

14

managed to learn about team spirit in my theatrical career.

It was at Brighton College that I met Christopher Hassall, who years later was to influence my decision to embark on a theatrical career. I don't quite know how Christopher and I became such firm friends. We were contemporaries and moved slowly up the school together. I liked his sense of humour. He was an unconventional sort of boy and didn't really fit in to the discipline of English public school life. He didn't take any particular notice of dramatic exploits of 'sandpiper knicks on Friday', as we called the Officer Training Course to which Brighton College was very loyal. It was a great school for getting up in khaki, shouldering a rifle and drilling. We were all little soldiers every Friday. Oh, those bloody puttees that had to be smoothly wound and of course wouldn't wind smoothly and were always overlapping the wrong way. Christopher was not very good at that sort of thing and had wonderful ways of getting out of Friday afternoon parades. I can't say I was madly keen but I obediently shouldered arms, did all sorts of things correctly and became an under-officer.

I got to know him better in the holidays when he took me to visit his father, the artist John Hassall, who was a remarkable and equally unconventional sort of chap. He had a cluttered studio in Notting Hill Gate in which nothing was allowed to be moved, dusted or thrown away and every spent tube of paint was treasured.

I have never concealed that, in those days, Brighton College was pretty poor academically though I'm prepared to believe it is a very good school now. A lot of the public schools were new then; they hadn't any real traditions and tended to make them up as they went along. Cricket and rugby-football were more important than the Classics. Brighton College was under the command of Canon Dawson, a very strong personality who was also a superb salesman. He expanded the school by at least two hundred per cent, so that it grew enormous. The bigger it became, of course, the worse the education. There was no time for individual scholastic encouragement. Thank God for Windlesham, my mother and Canon Hudson.

As I have mentioned, my mother had a great love of literature, especially poetry. She was a real Anglo-Indian, having absorbed the ethos of the British Raj during her time in India. She adored Kipling, reading him to us endlessly. She read to us marvellously and had a quotation for every occasion. This can be irritating and is a habit that I have unfortunately inherited.

She was a wonderful mother, not only to me and my two brothers but to Doody as well. She was tremendously affectionate in a formal way, particularly to me. She was a powerful woman, the power in the family really, which made the marriage tricky in its later years. She had a strong sense of duty and I suppose she was a bit austere and frightening to some people but not to me. I wonder sometimes whether she had a sense of humour. I remember on her birthday I gave her a *Just William* book. *Just William* was a passion of mine. I adored William's heroic qualities and longed to be like him, the chief of 'The Outlaws'. She practically never opened it and I don't think she read a word of it. I couldn't understand how anyone wouldn't find it absolutely riveting and terribly funny. It makes me laugh to this day but maybe *Just William* is an acquired taste. My disappointment at her reception of my gift has stayed with me all these years.

Mother had a far better brain than my father and was educated to a much higher standard. Poor Ned never read a book in his life. The basic thing I have to say about him is that I never really knew him. I never really met him until we went to live on Dartmoor. He was rather the *pater familias*, a hangover from Victorian family life. With his strict Anglican upbringing, he became known in his service days as 'Holy Jo'. He conducted family prayers at Haywards Heath. We all knelt down and prayed in the dining-room every morning. I don't

16

pray now and I can't find myself in tune with the Anglican service. My father would be horrified, less so my mother, although she was extremely God-fearing and disciplined in the faith. There were no family discussions about religion; God was God and that was that, and the *Bible* was the *Bible*. We were not a family who discussed things. Ned hardly talked to us at all. I regret to say that he didn't impinge much on my life.

CHAPTER 2

Dartmoor Days

It was in 1925, during my first term at Brighton College, that we moved from the comfortable suburbanity of Haywards Heath to a remote house on Dartmoor: called Jordan Manor. My parents saw an advertisement in *The Times* and Shrimp was despatched on his motorbike to look at the house. He was wild with excitement when he saw it and telephoned the parents to come and have a look. They went down to see it, agreed it was ideal and bought it for £800. I suppose the idea of the move was to experience real country. I also think it might have been a way of saving money.

The move to Dartmoor was a tremendous watershed in the family's history. Though it was to some extent a practical and economical step, it must have been very difficult for my parents. They had so little in common that I wonder what on earth drew them together in the first place. My father, Ned, was in many ways a very attractive man and of course their life in

India must have been glamorous and exciting, so I suppose that there must have been a certain chemistry between them. Yet going to live on Dartmoor and deliberately cutting themselves off from any real social life must have put a tremendous strain on them. They were thrown upon each other's company far more than before. I look back and wonder how on earth they survived it. It was thrilling for me, of course—everything a boy of fourteen could hope for—but there was no-one within anything like neighbourly reach with whom my parents could play bridge or enjoy social contact. There was no village. Jordan was a hamlet, the centre of which was our house, the manor house, and the mill with the waterwheel for grinding flour, which was run by Ernie Warren, white with flour from head to toe, who lived in the cottage opposite the mill.

My parents' sense of isolation must have increased even more because they were what we would call snobs. They were particularly careful about Doody mixing with 'a lower social class'. Looking back, it was a terrible attitude and very much isolated Doody. She was sent away to a boarding school in Somerset, which she loved. There was no question of any of us going to the local village school with the village children.

This awful snobbery is illustrated by the Massons. Next door to us in Jordan, and there wasn't much door to be next to, lived a very nice family called Masson. There were two little girls of Doody's age but any relationship between them was discouraged and, although they lived only fifty yards away, in ten years I never remember either of the two Masson children coming into Jordan Manor or my mother going to the Massons for a cup of sugar or some butter in a neighbourly way. They were not considered 'our class' because Mr Masson was a vet! It made no sense, but I'm afraid that was how the class system was in those days. This attitude was quite usual and it never occurred to us that there was anything odd about it. So there we were, poor as church mice, but terrible snobs.

I liked Mr Masson very much. He was a wonderful chap, a broad Scot, so nice and so good. He and I used to go fishing almost every night in the school holidays, trooping off into the woods, fishing for sea trout, and not once did he complain or refer to the situation. I had far more in common with Mr Masson, and more friendship and companionship, than I ever had with my father Ned.

Ned had no visible means of financial support, except, as I have already mentioned, his pension of £40 a month. That was not much on which to bring up a family. Having been in a senior rank in the Indian Marines, accustomed to servants and a private yacht, he must have found it difficult trying to look after four children, a wife and countless livestock on a very small income in an isolated house on Dartmoor. He must have pondered over it in his study at Jordan Manor into which he disappeared every morning with a huge cup of coffee and the previous day's copy of *The Times*. What did he do? To this day I don't know.

During our first summer on Dartmoor I couldn't be kept off the river. I learnt that sea trout (peal) ran up the Webburn and could be caught on a worm at night. Down in the woods, below Jordan, there was a pool on the river known locally as Head Weir Pool. I knew it as the Peal Pool and it was there that I would go with Mr Masson night after night in the summer holidays and rarely come home until the early hours without a sea trout or two. Sometimes there would be several of us at the pool; the Warrens, Nosworthys, Frenches and Chaffes. I recall precisely the sights, sounds and smells of those summer nights—boyhood magic.

I graduated to fly fishing and, thanks to my motorcycle, a two-stroke Francis-Barnett that I used to ride barefoot around the moor, my horizons widened dramatically. By day I got to know the wilder moorland streams, the East Dart, Swincombe, West Dart, Cherrybrook, Wallabrook. I was initiated into fly fishing for peal at night, a thrill which is with me still. Webburn Pool, Holme's Pool, Lower and Upper Corner Pools, the Wood Pools, Queenie Pool. Those were magic summer nights: the smell of honeysuckle wafting up out of the woods on the opposite bank, the whistles of the otters coming nearer and nearer by Comberstone Island, the sudden strong pull of a 5 lb sea trout. I developed a love of the moor that has never left me.

In the woods about Queenie Pool on the West Dart is a cave among the rocks known as Pixies Holt. There was a pincushion in the cave with a fishing fly hooked in it. It was supposed to bring luck from the pixies. Mine, placed there over sixty years ago, certainly has brought me luck; I wonder whether it is still there.

A great many alterations had to be done to the house before we could live in it. It was a Dartmoor longhouse, designed to be lived in by people and animals under one roof. Cow-byres had to be turned into rooms and the roof rethatched. But it remained primitive, with no electricity and only oil for cooking and lighting. How Mother worked. I always think of her with flour on her face. She must have been a very good cook, not an extravagant one, and would rustle up amazing family meals, cooking Christmas dinner under the most appalling circumstances on a tiny Valor Perfection oil stove!

Mother was helped in the house for several years by Miss Costello, an Irish lady we found through *The Church Times*. Very Irish, she never swept the floor, she 'twigged it', and milk that went sour had 'cracked'. We always called her, very formally, Miss Costello, although she was really one of the family. Eventually, she left and ran a tea shop in Hythe.

Mother was also helped by the Admiral, an ex-naval rating who lived two miles away in Lower Ponsworthy and came over twice a week to help with the garden and do the washing up and any odd jobs. Then there was Mrs Warren, who came every day to do the rough work. In the last letter that Mother ever wrote, she said that 'we are having trouble because the Admiral says Ned is paying too much attention to Mrs Warren'.

There were no telephones on Dartmoor. The Post Office agreed that, if we could collect seven subscribers, they would put in an exchange. We managed to round up enough residents and were given the exchange. We were Poundsgate 4. The post office was run by a very nice couple called Fred and Lillian Bamsey. The whole exchange was bubbling. I don't understand telegraphy, but each subscriber had to have a different number of rings. So, as soon as the telephone rang, all conversation stopped in the home whilst we counted the number of rings. Of course, we often got it wrong and someone would already be on the phone having a private conversation. Fred and Lillian had a loudspeaker in their living room and, I suspect, knew a thing or two about what was happening in the district.

The postal system was remarkable. The lovely thing about it was the old postman called Mr Avery who, when we bought the house, was actually living in the back of it with his mad wife. When we moved into the house we took them on as sitting tenants, which is why we got the house so cheaply, I suppose. They were living in the kitchen and had a bedroom above the horses, sleeping in the hay in the stables, a cosy but smelly arrangement. It must have stunk like old boots. Doody remembers coming into the kitchen to find the postman's awful old wife, whom we thought was a witch, cutting her husband's toenails on the kitchen table! He was stone deaf. If you wanted to talk to him you had to go right up to his ear, which was always filthy, and shout into it. This wonderful old boy walked at least seventeen miles on his rounds every day except Sunday, walking down the middle of the road, unable to hear a thing. Eventually, Dr Steele, the local doctor, built them a bungalow on the other side of the river where we couldn't smell them. On summer evenings, the old postman would sit on the steps of his hut, playing the penny whistle, which he loved although he couldn't hear it, and they were very happy there for the rest of their lives.

There was also a good deal of livestock to take care of. Chickens were my father's contribution to the household. We brought back wild duck eggs from the marshland and set them under hens so we had quite a large population of mallard living around the house. When Mother came down in the morning to open 'up', the house was suddenly full of ducks which all came in through the windows. In the breeding season, they made their nests down by the Webburn, and the drakes would go down to the ducks and lead them up to the house for feeding. Falling over in their excitement they would waddle after us all through the house. We loved them, and never ate them.

The porch of Jordan always smelt awful, which must have been very off-putting for visitors who were not used to us. The smell came from the worms we used to collect for fishing. We got them from the moor, under peat where it had been cut and laid out to dry; under each cutting would be great, big, lovely worms. We ate a good deal of fish at Jordan and there were always fresh fish hanging from a hook in the kitchen. We had two dogs, a lovely bitch called Treacle Tart and a stupid cocker spaniel, inappropriately named Mirth, that someone had given us as a gun dog. She was gun shy and would run off in the opposite direction as soon as she heard a shot. The cats and dogs used to have their children in a cosy cupboard next to the dining room fireplace and, puppies or kittens regardless, they were all mothered by Treacle Tart. Father had a horse called Jimbo. We all had a go at riding and I hunted a bit with the South Devon, which I enjoyed very much. There was also a beastly little pony called Chloe which my father had bought for Doody. It turned out to be a very bad-tempered, unfriendly animal, which went mad when you tried to ride it.

When we went fishing Doody would tag behind us with her homemade rod and a fly made out of a turkey feather and a piece of Chloe's tail. We were a noisy lot, quite witty and rather cruel, and must have been rather overwhelming for Doody, who was under the impression that she was rather dim. This idea was reinforced by us boys cruelly mocking her when her school reports were read out: 'Poor Doody, she can't help it, her brain is divided into three,' we used to say. Years later, after Mother's death, Doody devotedly cared for my father for a good many years. He insisted it was her duty to do so as he had saved her by kindly bringing her into the family. Thank God for the war. She finally managed to escape and join the war effort.

I was away at school during term time but came home for the holidays, travelling on the Great Western Railway. I used to take a taxi across London to Paddington, and I felt a real swell having lunch on the train, which cost five shillings. I had saved up for some time to have this wonderful meal and I remember little biscuit tins being brought round, and water-cress. I would be met at Newton Abbot, or sometimes Exeter, by Ned and Doody in the Morris Cowley tourer which Ned (who was the worst driver ever to sit behind a steering wheel) used to drive around the moor in a frightening fashion. He was under the impression that everything would be all right as long as he blew the horn loud enough, which he would do when he came out of the little lane from our house on to the main road, never slowing down for an instant.

Once a week, we would go shopping in Ashburton or, if we were feeling particularly adventurous, Newton Abbot, but that was about the extent of our motoring. The old Morris would go backwards up some of the hills, reverse gear being lower than bottom.

Those holidays seemed to go on forever and were wonderful—fishing, ponies and riding and my motorcycle. Winters were very bleak on Dartmoor, but wonderful. There were no winter sports—Dartmoor is no place for skiing—but it was exhilarating to walk or ride about the cold, wild moor. There is an umbilical cord between me and the moor. At that time, it was like being in love; it is an inexplicable feeling, and the whole atmosphere of the place calls me back to it.

And then there was the business of the bees. Ned decided we ought to have bees and obtained three hives from Buckfast Abbey. I don't know much about bees but I understand that the popular bee nowadays is the fairly quiet Italian bee. We had the Old English Black Bee and he is a bugger.

On the whole, I tried to keep out of it all, but I understand that one thing bees hate is being dealt with on a hot day and definitely not on a Sunday. They are quite particular about this. We had our three hives in the top field and Ned, who had a heart condition and was not supposed to lift heavy weights, decided, one hot August Sunday, to take the honey. As he lifted the excluder from the hive, there was an appalling weight of honey. As he staggered, he knocked the hive and the bees came out to remonstrate. Ned, being the splendid, brave sailor and all that, was determined not to let go of the honey harvest until he had got to the shed where he kept all his bee things. So he carried the honey, being stung all the way.

It was the summer holidays and we were all there. His brave sons rushed down to the river and plunged in up to their noses. We were the only living things in the area to escape being stung. There was absolute pandemonium. Chickens were screaming and dashing hither and thither. Turkeys dropped down dead and the Buzzard, which we had found wounded on the moor and which was living peacefully in the dog kennel, was killed. It was quite a do. All the animals, with their tails up or down or between their legs, were dashing round the countryside screaming. My dear father came up to the house in the middle of all this chaos and Mother yelled from an upstairs window, 'Ned, take your clothes off in the garden', which he did. They were like a hive full of bees. When he came in, she picked a hundred and fifty stings out of him. He swelled up to twice his size and turned black. The doctor came and it was touch and go for about twenty-four hours. Afterwards, he used to say that that was the end of his rheumatism.

It was around this time that my brother Shrimp had an affair that completely altered the direction of his life. Shrimp was the brains of the family and when he left Brighton College he went up to Oxford to read Spanish. In his third year at Oxford he met, and fell in love with, a beautiful woman called Dacia Stuart Robinson. Unfortunately, Dacia was already married, with three small children. Her husband was Stuart Robinson, known as Wob, a farmer who was something of a figure in the county of Herefordshire and also something of an eccentric. He had a habit of paying Dacia, by the hour, to tickle his feet. It soon became obvious that the liaison between Shrimp and Dacia was impossible. Shrimp felt that the only thing he could do was to remove himself from the situation and so, just one term away from sitting his finals, he upped and went to India as a tea planter, briefly becoming engaged on the rebound to a young woman he met on the boat going over.

Shrimp stayed in India for five years, after which time he returned to England and almost immediately went to see Dacia. This shook the family up properly. My mother had been very fond of Dacia and had no real idea of the depth of feeling between them. The episode wounded her deeply when she realized the truth. I was not worried by the morals of it all. I was very fond of Dacia. She was a lovable creature, and comely moreover. I was on their side.

Dacia's husband was also a most successful breeder of Herefordshire cattle, winning top prizes at the Royal Show. Eventually his interest in Herefordshire cattle waned and he took to growing prize sweetpeas and miniature gladioli. Together with Dacia, who was very good at flower arranging, they did very well, winning prizes at all the shows. Then he made the mistake of going into sheep breeding, bringing Kerry Hill sheep down to his luscious cattle-breeding farm in Herefordshire. Not being used to such a rich diet, they blew up and died and soon he was surrounded by dead animals. This, combined with the 1930s slump, collapsing investments and three children to educate, proved too much for him and one night, in despair, he took an overdose of laudanum. Dacia called the doctor and together they worked furiously all night to pull him through. In those days suicide was a criminal offence, so the police had to be informed; poor Wob was sent to a mental home, where he stayed for six months, obviously in a terrible state of depression. Eventually, he was allowed out with instructions that on no account should he be left alone. One day, whilst walking around the estate, he gave his companion the slip and committed suicide by throwing himself off a silage tower.

Shrimp, meanwhile, had moved into a converted railway carriage in the garden, where he brewed up a secret recipe for floor polish which he had bought from a man he met on a journey. The man convinced him that this amazing polish would make his fortune; he had some success with it, driving round to schools and institutions and selling vast drums of it.

Some time after Wob's death, when things had calmed down a little, Shrimp and Dacia set up home together. They were unable to marry because of a clause in Wob's will stating, rather unkindly, that there would be no more money for Dacia if

27

she remarried. They stayed together for twenty years before eventually separating. During that time, Shrimp tried his hand at several ventures—a chicken farm, pigs, a kitchen garden. He adored the pigs and used to go and tell them all his troubles, years later, when love had grown cold and Dacia was being horrid to him.

Shrimp now lives a cheerful bachelor existence in Great Bedwyn, near my cottage in Berkshire. We still go fishing together. He is now stone deaf and I tend to fall over, but we enjoy ourselves. We must make a funny couple, shouting to each other on the riverbank. In my fishing diary for January 1931 I wrote:

It seems queer to be writing this in midwinter but here I am. I came down to Sussex for a pleasant interview with the dentist, having had raging toothache all the weekend of the final trial at Twickenham where Peter was playing. I stayed at Windlesham for a day and a night and went over to Steyning and fished with Gordon [Lyon]. I have come to the conclusion that there is an awful lot in coarse fishing chiefly as Gordon is so frightfully keen. We went out on a gorgeous frosty morning in his car to a pond (heaven knows where) to fish for pike. When we got there the water was frozen tight and we couldn't even move the punts. As the day was so absolutely marvellous we didn't seem to feel disappointed but went onto the Arun at Stopham Bridge. We didn't catch a fish all day but I've never been so glad that I was a fisherman. It was an absolutely marvellous day to start with and secondly I'd never spun properly before, that's to say with a spinning rod and reel, and it was a marvellous feeling being able to throw a bait and see it come to the water 40 or 50 yards away at the other side of the river. I never felt a suspicion of a fish all day. All the low-lying land around the banks had had a sheet of ice over it here and there sort of bridging little dykes and hollows and all day for some reason this was cracking and going off with a sound like gunshots and as I moved along way upstream away from everybody and everything it was most eerie; all the time the sun was behind a haze which next day turned to snow but which made the sun a blood colour that got deeper as the day grew later. In the end I underestimated my own capabilities and caught the opposite bank. By the enormous strain I had to put on before the line broke I judged that it would have to be a pretty heavy pike to break away. Gordon was in awfully good form and seemed very well and we got about marvellously although neither of us had any luck. I'm sure we have seldom enjoyed a day as well. There were lots of birds on the frozen marshes. I saw plenty of snipe and duck and plover. I must take up spinning seriously. I've managed to get a job at Beaconsfield and term begins on January 23rd.

I began writing my fishing diary in a large thick exercise book bought at 'Gillett's Stationers and Printers, Market Street, Brighton', in 1929. I have kept it for the last forty years just for the sake of statistics, conditions, weight of fish, fly used, etc. It tells a few lies in pen and ink, but most of it is for my eyes only and I have it in my will that it must be destroyed upon my demise. So I am rather coy of showing it to the world, but it was an important part of my life and, besides very many technicalities of interest only to the dedicated fisherman, it contains a few anecdotes and observations about people as well as fish.

When I eventually left Brighton College, I had to look around for something to do and the only thing that suggested itself to me was schoolmastering. I got a job at a prep school in

Beaconsfield called Norfolk House. It was run by a frightful woman whom I called Mrs Tarvin, after the wife of the head-master in J. B. Priestley's *The Good Companions*. She ruled the place with a rod of iron and was an absolute bitch. I kept my head down and hoped she wouldn't notice what a hopeless schoolmaster I was. I romantically saw myself dealing with my difficulties with the easy, indolent charm of an Inigo Jollifant.

It was during these abortive Beaconsfield schoolmastering days that I joined my first 'grown-up' amateur company and found myself in the finals of a British Drama League competition with a play called *Ritzio's Boots*. Playing the hero, Ritzio, I was discovered behind a curtain in the queen's bedroom and run through with a sword, like Polonius. The finals of this event were held at Welwyn Garden City. There were four plays a night for a week, twenty-four in all. To our great surprise and mortification, *Ritzio's Boots* had no success at all and the play that walked off with all the prizes was something called *Not This Man* by one Sydney Box. This play won every single prize: best acted, best written, best dressed, etc, etc. It was highly acclaimed by everyone but me. I suppose that, in an ungraceful fit of sour grapes, I wanted to be the one dissenting voice. Egged on by my friends and probably rather perversely, I wrote a letter to *The Welwyn Times*, saying that I considered the play to be blasphemous bunk and cheap theatrical claptrap. Days later, my landlady announced a Mr Box to see me and there, standing in the garden, was a very large man who turned out to be Sydney Box's brother. Tapping me on the shoulder with an official-looking document, he said, 'I think you might be expecting this'. Still not knowing what was in the wind, I read 'King George V, by the grace of God, Emperor of India, defender of the faith of Great Britain and Ireland and dominions beyond the seas. To Michael Hordern of 20, Julians Road . . . Greetings'. I read on. It was a writ for libel. I had accused Sydney Box of the most heinous of crimes, blasphemy.

Once I had stopped laughing and realized the seriousness of it all, I managed to find a splendidly old fashioned firm of solicitors called Bull and Bull in Lincoln's Inn. They were delighted to act for me. They were the family of the actor, Peter Bull, and have been my solicitors ever since. The case came up in the High Court of Justice in Lincoln's Inn before Mr Justice Talbot and a special jury. It was quite a number. I shared the front page of *The Evening Standard* with Mussolini. Wisely—very wisely as it turned out, as I would have condemned myself out of my own mouth—my counsel did not put me in the box. We won the case and it didn't cost me a penny, but it cost Sydney Box a great deal. Years later, when I was in a film he was producing at British Lion in Shepherd's Bush, I met him for the first time. 'You absolutely broke me,' he said. 'I paid it back in twelve monthly instalments, but it was marvellous publicity and really started my career.'

By the Easter holidays, I was back in Devon, getting some interesting fishing done on the water of Major Cooke-Hurle, who with his wife much resembled a brace of pheasant! In my fishing diary for 1931, I wrote:

Rather a poor holiday as far as fishing is concerned. Margaret somehow got round Major Cooke-Hurle for me and I had every Tuesday on his water during April and only got two keepable fish the whole time. The stream itself, the Bovey, is supposed to be one of the best in Devon but the Major thinks of little but his pheasants which he VERY closely resembles, and his water, though no doubt excellent, is very much overgrown. He is very particular about who he lets fish(!), however, and I am looking forward to first-rate sport. To start with the weather was against me every time—no really it was—snowing on one occasion and always with a cold downstream wind. There's one marvellous pool above a weir where I got my two fish one day when the sun was out and I saw some more good fish in it. I went to dinner at the Hurles one night and down his end of the table there's a stuffed cock pheasant and up hers a hen and all four looked so incredibly alike that I couldn't take my eyes off them.

My efforts at schoolmastering had lasted only a term, during which time I had to do all sorts of awful things like play cricket. In spite of my inadequacies as a teacher, I am proud to say that one of my pupils got the top scholarship to Marlborough. Polio, thank goodness, took me out of it all. This ghastly occurrence, unpleasant though it was, gave me time to reflect and, as I lay on my bed of sickness, suffering from 'acute anterior poliomyelitis', I realized I was barking up the wrong tree. Teaching would have been a complete dead end as a career. I had no degree, no right to be there at all. I would never have earned any money.

The polio episode happened after the Otter Hunt Ball at the Two Bridges Hotel near Princetown. I had driven the old open Morris Cowley over to the Two Bridges, danced the night away and got terribly hot. Feeling peculiar, and obviously running a high temperature, I drove back across the moors in the early hours. The next morning, I couldn't get out of bed. The doctor was called, there was a great deal of alarm and jumping up and down, and I was out of action for the entire summer and most of the winter.

I did manage to persuade the doctor to let me go fishing on the last day of the salmon season. Taking my poor mother up to Dartmeet, we went to a pool called Coombe Weir and there, trembling in every limb, I hooked my first salmon. The excitement was too much for me of course and the bloody thing got off. I sat down, grown person that I was, and cried my eyes out. It was not until three years after my mother had died that I did at last catch my first salmon.

It was on 12 June 1935, on the right bank down by Eagle Rock: a 10 lb salmon. So thrilled and excited, so proud was I, I carried it upstream and waded across the river below Dartmeet, ostentatiously crossing the river hoping to meet as many tourists as possible at Badgers Holt on the opposite bank.

My precious fishing diary records that memorable day:

It seems a shame that this entry is not made in red ink. I've caught my first salmon! And on the Dart too. The Brownriggs lent us Wild Goose for the week and Shrimp and Dacia and a girlfriend of D's and a man friend of S's and I occupied the cottage for a misty heavenly week. Major Cooke-Hurle kindly gave me a day on his water and on that great day, Wednesday June 12th I got into a salmon in the flats above Eagles Rock. It was a thrill to wait all these years for my knees knocked and my heart thumped and I felt so ill that for some time I honestly wished I had never hooked it. I could see myself weeping beside a broken cast in ten minutes' time and I knew how I should feel but I gave the fish hell and the butt and in about 7 minutes I had my gaff out but he saw it and fled; with the gaff between my teeth, looking and swearing like a pirate, I played him for another 2 or 3 minutes. I wish I could have seen and heard myself. Then he was on the bank and 'Michael Hordern,' I said in a loud voice 'has killed a salmon' and I wanted very badly to cry as I used to when I got good fish. I was too thrilled to go on fishing but picked up the fish and hurried back to Dartmeet. I waded across the Dart at one place at great risk to life, limb, rod and salmon just for the pleasure of impressing two trippers on the opposite bank. I succeeded. 'Coo,' they said as I went by, 'what is it?' 'Oh,' I said nonchalantly 'a salmon, you know'.

Mrs Cross [who kept the filling station at Dartmeet] embraced me voluminously and was as pleased as I was. Not the least pleasant part of it was the 'shloop' noise it made as it fell on the granite floor of Wild Goose, a noise that I had so often hoped to hear at Jordan. The photographs Mrs Cross took of me dishevelled, triumphant and holding my ten-pounder unfortunately never came out but the ones that Dacia took of me next day did.

The rest of the week was grand but of course pale in comparison. The Wallabrook, the Webburn again (what a topping stream) and the Stewes Coxes water on the East Dart scene of former triumphs. On the latter I got a fine trout of just a pound and S and P on the whole did very well in other old haunts. Dartmoor fish may be small but my God they're the best that swim. It was a misty week and when the mist lifted it rained. But every evening we drew chairs round a roaring open log fire, and woodsmoke and beer and the mist at the window felt like home again.

Winnie, Dacia's cook, was with us and I think she will always remember the ceremony of cooking my first salmon—in fact that holiday without Winnie to look after us would not have been the same.

We had always made a big thing of Christmas at Jordan. There was Holy Communion on Christmas morning. (We went to church every Sunday; we were great God botherers.) Then the little heaps of presents which were a great feature and, of course, Christmas dinner, cooked miraculously on the four burner Valor Perfection. The spirit of those times comes over in this extract from a letter Mother wrote to Shrimp.

December 30th, 1932.

We have had a week of it and I can hardly believe all the rush is over. Just the ordinary life starting up again. [*Immediately after this she took to her bed, never to get up again.*] It's all been lovely, especially Michael's party, of which I enjoyed every second, except for wishing you could be there too. We had seven failures, the Skewes-Cox's had flu, Major Fletcher had a bad head and Margaret Fox had tummy ache. However, the Dowsens, Andersons, Joan Partridge and Keith came and Hooks Huntingdon came for the hunt ball and stayed on and was excellent value. He and Tommy carried all before them in the competitions which were a terrible brain storm. Peter and Michael arranged them all and the whole show went with a magnificent swing. Such a lot of noise. I am always amazed at the marvellous hoots my family, including Doody, made. Peter disappeared for a bit, before the interval, and when we went in for refreshments there were wonderful scrambled eggs and plates warming on the stove, to my great surprise. We had various kinds of rather exotic sandwiches, cheese straws, salted almonds, various desserts, orange and grape-fruit, beer, sherry, lemonade, coffee on arrival, tea about one, after which they left in a downpour.

In January 1933, my poor mother died. She was only fifty-nine and died from exhaustion. She had been a marvellous mother but she had had a hard-working, worrying time trying to rear the four of us properly. It wasn't an easy house to live in and I think she had had enough. Shrimp recently found a letter, which she sent to him a week or two before she died. I think it gives a very good idea of some of the problems she had to contend with. This is an extract from it.

Doody fell victim yesterday, having nursed me and done all the outside jobs, and has moved in to be near the fire and had a temperature of 103. Mine normal, so I hope to be up tomorrow. Poor Michael, with a streaming cold, is the sole survivor, Ned being a walking case, says he aches in every bone and has, as usual, got it in the lungs, where he never had an illness yet. To add to all our woes, the oil stove won't function and, on this wet and awful morning, Michael must spend hours in the back yard dealing with it. The car dynamo has also gone phut, halleluja. Poor Tommy has been very bad (Peter's first girlfriend). Eva (doctor) has just been, says Ned is in for it, his temperature is rising and he must go to bed in your room, poor Michael. She is firm with me not leaving my bed. She suggests we try to get Dorcas to sleep in. [*Dorcas lived in the village and used to come and do.*] Dorcas has had a frightful cold and isn't allowed in here. What luck we do have. Now the bathroom pipes have burst, flooding everywhere and Michael said the oil stove is full of water. What can be done?

All her brave sons were with her when she died. When it was over, we did the most extraordinary thing. We went downstairs, opened one of the bottles of champagne which had been prescribed by the doctor, turned on the wireless and listened to *The Billy Cotton Band Show*. What poor Ned must have been feeling didn't bother us at all. The church couldn't hold all the people at her funeral.

After mother's death I spent a long convalescence dreamily wandering about the moor, sometimes being joined in my wanderings by Mrs Kathleen Bailey, a splendid upstanding woman about six feet tall, her lovely labrador and Delia. Delia was a white ferret who lived in Delia's castle, a large and comfortable hutch, and accompanied Mrs Bailey on these walks wearing a collar and a long piece of string for extricating her from rabbit holes. Taking no offence at this, Delia would cheerfully continue her walk.

On Dartmoor, Kathleen Bailey must have seemed a strange figure, striding across the moors with Delia. She was not a very successful fisherperson, but she fished with great enthusiasm and I would gilly for her. Her husband was a small, retiring man. They were pleased to be back in England, having just retired from a lifetime in Kenya shooting every game animal it was possible to shoot except one particular horned creature whose name I have forgotten but whose escape from their gun was a constant source of regret to them. They had moved into Cator Court, a large Victorian Gothic house whose rooms were filled with the results of their labours. Rhinos, lions, elephants gazed down from every wall and on Kathleen's desk was a large rhino horn around which long golden tresses of human hair protruded, still attached to a shrivelled piece of scalp. This was a puzzle to me until, one day, Kathleen lifted up the hair on the side of her head and showed me a large bald patch where she had been literally scalped. The story was that one day in the bush she had shot a rhino which, instead of obligingly dropping down dead, had charged furiously. I understand that the correct procedure in this sort of rhino-hunting situation is to stand absolutely still until exactly the right moment, when the lumbering ton of rhino is almost upon you, and then step sharply to the side. Showing a good deal of courage, Kathleen held her ground, only leaping to the side at the very last moment. She mistimed the move by a fraction of a second; the rhino, charging past, knocked her out, its horn dragging a good deal of hair from her head before it finally dropped down dead.

When Kathleen came round, she discovered to her horror

37

and dismay that the dead rhino had been protecting her calf. Hurt and distressed that she should have killed this baby's mother, Kathleen and the bearer took the calf back to the house, where she carefully nursed it. She would push a milk-soaked sponge on a long pole through the bars of the cage, gradually shortening the length of the pole each day until the rhino was eating out of her hand. Every day she would sit and read it fairy stories so that it should become used to the human voice. In this way she managed to rear the baby, which she called Kathleen.

Eventually, the time came for the Baileys to leave Kenya. What to do with Kathleen? Realizing the rhino would never survive in the wild, she decided to give it to London Zoo and there she lived for many years with a plate above her cage, 'Kathleen donated by Mrs Kathleen Bailey'.

Some years later, when she was in England, Kathleen visited Kathleen. On seeing her the rhino went mad with joy and excitement. Persuading the keeper, much against his will, to let her into the cage, the enormous creature went up to her, lay down and put its head in her lap as it used to do when it was a baby all those years ago. It was so traumatic that Kathleen could never go back again. I was very moved when I saw this creature, thinking of its previous life, the milk-soaked sponge and the nursery rhymes.

CHAPTER 3

A Stage Career in Sight

Johnny Appleton, an old chum from Windlesham who was on holiday near Dartmoor, cheerfully suggested that when, or if, I ever recovered from the terrible polio, I might think about joining his family firm, the Educational Supply Association. As I was only too glad to have a chance to get on with life and earn some money, I gratefully agreed.

The ESA was a very popular outfit supplying schools all over the country with all the things schools need; desks, blackboards, chalk, everything. They decided that I should work in each of their various departments in turn. At their own furniture factory in Stevenage, I started working on the machines, battling away with lathes and screwdrivers. I remember the peculiar and lovely smell of timber. I moved on to selling, driving around the absolute plum areas of Sussex and Kent in my small Rover. I enjoyed this. There is a lot of similarity between selling and acting, and I was happy.

Whilst making school desks at Stevenage, I joined an amateur dramatics company. We performed in the town hall. I did two plays with them, one as lieutenant Raleigh in *Journey's End* and the other an old-fashioned play called *Diplomacy*, which was a good deal more old-fashioned by the time we had done with it. This was my first experience of the 'cue' script— strange idea, the purpose of which I never really understood unless it was one of economy. A master copy of one entire script would be printed, and the other scripts would be made of cue lines, each character getting the appropriate cues and lines. This was all very confusing as you had no idea whether the speech ahead of you was three pages long or only one line, but once you rehearsed and put the lines together you soon got the hang of it. It was rather good in a way as it really made you listen to what each character was saying.

Through the Stevenage amdrams I became great friends with a local family called Grosvenor. The father was the local GP in Stevenage. He was very old-fashioned; he didn't have a stethoscope but used a trumpet. He lived with his daughter, Dorothy, an exceptionally plain girl with a strange trick of blowing her hair out of her eyes all the time. She was an extremely kind woman and everyone adored her. She was a very keen amdram, always playing everybody's mother. Her handsome brother, Chetwynd Grosvenor, also a doctor, was adored by all the ladies in the district, but he had no time for amdrams. He went hunting, fishing and shooting, country pursuits that in those days you could follow in Stevenage. We used to go fishing together. In the summer of 1933 I wrote this:

The day on the Collinsplatt's water was just marvellous and the best day's fishing I've ever had, quite. I took my lunch and started about eleven o'clock. I'd had four trout and was up at a tiny pool above an island towards the end of their water when I saw a fish of some 2–3 lbs—yes 2–3 lbs I said—rising steadily off a stone off the top end of the island. I watched him carefully and put my fly right over him. I was trembling so much but even then I found time to wonder how I did such a good cast, he took it just as he should have done and I struck just as I should have done—perfect—I saw myself landing the record trout of the year but the fish thought otherwise and made off downstream, I got in after him prepared to follow him down to the sea but again he decided that was a bad thing and leapt into a bush—finish. I got onto the bank and stared at the broken gut, but didn't cry—I must be growing up—I wish I could have done, it might have relieved me.

In the summer, I joined an out-of-door company and played Shakespeare on the lawns of country houses. I played Orlando in *As You Like It* and thought myself very dashing. Playing opposite me in *Love's Labour's Lost* the part of Don Amado (a part I played at Stratford years later) was a man called Osmond Daltry, who later put his money into theatrical management. He was to offer me my first professional job and introduce me to yet another very important man in my life, Patrick Ide.

I had also joined an amateur dramatic society in London: the St Pancras People's Theatre. It was based in an old deconsecrated Wesleyan chapel in St Pancras and was a very superior amateur Old Vic run by a splendid lady called Edith Neville, who was a friend of Lilian Baylis and who made made us work very hard and properly, almost as one would in a professional repertory season. I took this very seriously. I would be selling exercise books in Ramsgate or Margate, look at my watch and think 'Oh God, I've got rehearsal at half past six . . .', let in my clutch and come screaming back to London.

It was obvious after some time that this could not go on. I had been with the firm about five years and was being groomed

41

for stardom; I was about to go into the offices and maybe become a director. But I was spending so much time on my theatricals with the amdrams that I really thought I must come clean with Johnny Appleton's father, who had been so kind to me. Did I intend to become a professional actor, he asked. I thought for a moment and said 'Yes, I suppose I do.' Typically, he couldn't have been more helpful. He was very complimentary about my efforts over the last five years and said I could stay with the firm until I found a job in the theatre. When I finally decided to leave the ESA, I took my replacement round my patch of Sussex and Kent and introduced him to the vagaries of selling exercise books. Then off I went in search of my first professional theatrical job.

By this time, I had a little room above a snack bar in Porchester Place by Marble Arch. I ate in the snack bar, which was run by a lovely ex-army man. Any free time I had had between selling school exercise books and the amdrams was spent in the company of the Partridges, three beautiful girls— Joan, Betty and Bobby—who lived in Hampstead. We used to go dancing together. I was still very much involved in the St Pancras People's Theatre, and it was partly this company that made me make up my mind to throw in my lot and become an actor.

Here is an extract from a cheerful letter I wrote to dear Dorothy Grosvenor which illustrates the state of Euphoria I was in at that time. Life was fun. I was thoroughly enjoying myself. My future lay in theatre.

> 23, Cambridge St
> London W.2
> 6.11.36

My Dear Dor
Assuming the voice of rumour has not yet reached you (and knowing Stevenage's capacity for same I think it

most unlikely that it hasn't) I beg to inform you, as we used to say when I was in business! I have resigned from the ESA and am going on the stage and to people who may say to you 'oh yes he was all very fine in local amateur shows but let him wait till he turns pro: and then we will see how good he is!' You may say that I'm not doing it because I THINK I'm good but because I KNOW I'm keen.

Many and various are my reasons for doing it but it boils down to this. I haven't got time for both my acting and my job and knowing that if I kept to the job I would have spent the rest of my life cursing myself for not at least TRYING the stage when I was young enough to fail and start again, I decided to say goodbye to the ESA.

I expect to start whatever I do (it may be a dramatic school for a year) in the New Year and the firm said stay with us as long as you can and as long as you like and just let us know when you're fixed up, so I shall be with them for another month or so.

I have already given up my car, which is a pretty nasty wrench, but I feel much better for having to walk so where's the loss? I used it for the last time last weekend and spent it rushing round first to Pa in Bath then to one brother in Hereford and then another at Bromsgrove, and they all said 'Well we all knew it would happen one day!' or words to that effect. So that was alright. Then I went to some friends to borrow £300 as I thought it would be cheaper than solicitors (to live on and pay for my training) and they said '"Loan oft loseth both itself and friend". We won't even lend you a £1 but we'll give you £50.' So that was alright! However I may not even need that as several kind London friends are doing their best to pull strings and so I might get a repertory job straight away though I am under no misapprehensions about my

43

faults and am quite prepared to have to train.

Anyway, be all that as it may, it is a great relief to be able to say Goodbye to the commercial traveller. At the moment I am being driven round the countryside by my successor, introducing him to my customers, and I find it a very pleasant and irresponsible occupation. I am also hard at rehearsals for *Distinguished Gathering* at St P. at the end of next week. Which except for the pantomime at Christmas will (God willing) be 'positively my last appearance' as an amateur! So that's that and I felt you might be amused.

My love to your father, Chetwynd and Therese.

Yours
Michael

P.S. God knows when I shall throw a trout fly again though!

Another influence in my decision to become a professional actor was my old friend from Brighton College, Christopher Hassall. He always called me Nabbath after my family motto (instituted, I think, in the Victorian era), *Nabbath hig Hordern ac God hic Fett*', which apparently means 'We have no storehouse. God will provide'. 'Hordern' is Anglo-Saxon for 'storehouse', hence 'to hoard'. For some reason which escapes me, I always called Christopher, George.

Christopher had gone up to Wadham College, Oxford, and joined the Oxford University Dramatic Society. He was very highly thought of, playing Romeo opposite Peggy Ashcroft's Juliet, directed by John Gielgud. The production later came up to London to the New Theatre, where I went to see my old chum playing Romeo. He was very 'in' with the theatre and went on to play small parts at the Old Vic, but his strong suit was obviously writing. He became very friendly with Ivor

Novello and wrote many of the lyrics for his musical shows.

Amongst the theatrical people Christopher took up with was a very distinguished civil servant, Edward Marsh, who was a great enthusiast for the arts, especially the theatre. They both came down to see me at the St Pancras People's Theatre in *Distinguished Gathering*, a popular West End play of the time. I felt it was a great honour to be assessed by Eddie Marsh, who apparently approved of my performance. I wrote a ridiculously over-humble letter to Christopher apologizing for being such a terrible amdram actor and received, by return, this wonderful letter, which set my mind to seek a career on the stage.

Nabbath hig Hordern ac God hic Fett
We have no storehouse, God will provide.

My Dear Nabbath
I had barely dipped my pen to write you a critical eulogy when I got your absurdly apologetic letter. I enjoyed the play enormously, and my tame celebrity, Edward Marsh, (who, by the way, is one of the best experts on the theatre of our time) was also delighted. I mean that; he was genuinely impressed with your performance. You're a damn fool to be apologetic.

Quite frankly, I was pleasantly surprised. Considering your small experience, I never expected you would be able to 'move' so well on the stage. You have fortunately a slim figure, agile, and normal feet. (A few of the company had very obstrusive feet.) To walk about the stage is supposed to be the first and hardest lesson for the actor. John Gielgud made me walk up and down a single plank on the floor of his studio to make me keep my feet parallel. Your appearance is all in your favour. Your voice, though good and clear, wants to have a bit more urgency. Mr Marsh would not agree with me on that. I don't mean pitch or loudness or diction; it is a mental quality, a kind of exaggerated sincerity (that's a good phrase) that the stage requires. I would like to feel a stronger impetus, an underlying 'nervous tension' even in the most trivial subordinate scene. I know I'm right about this. It is a criticism only a 'pro' would make, because, as I say, with your speaking there is no superficial facet to be found. Owen Nares, a typical drawing-room actor, whose sort of part you were playing, 'throws away' lines and behaves in a convincingly casual and effortless fashion on the stage, but behind it all, underneath it, is a very powerful concentration—which to the professional actor soon becomes instinctive and habitual, and not an effort as you would first feel it to be. It is this mental quality, which keeps your attention riveted. You would be surprised to learn how much an actor's psychological reactions are felt by an audience, quite apart from his words and gestures. Owen Nares gives the illusion of being perfectly natural, but it is actually 'exaggerated sincerity' which brings him into focus with the audience. Now your performance had gone beyond the amateur state, which finds it difficult to be at ease and natural before an audience. There was a complete self-confidence about you, you spoke the lines unaffectedly, you moved gracefully, on the stage, though it was obviously you who was the temporary scene of interest. The times were not many, but they did occur, and they were nothing to do with your acting as such. It was just that you were taking the situation in your stride, letting your memory of the words and desire to be natural, carry you along. It was an occasional lack of exaggerated sincerity and sort of deep-down tenseness. If you disagree or don't follow me, we must have the question out face to face. I make a lot of it, not because it was noticeable to any degree, but because it was the only thing, a subtle thing too, that prevented your performance from being quite professional. From the ordinary Academy of Dramatic Art point of view, that is the superficially critical point of view, my only censure concerns your hands, that were clasped a little too often in front of you. You hardly ever just let them hang at your side. Go and study the actor C.V. France for that sort of thing. It seemed to come as a relief to you, when you held the rolled-up manuscript in your hand and could punctuate your sentences with it, so to speak. That is the only criticism the man in the street would make, but the point I would like to emphasize is one I would only make if I felt as I do, that it was worth aiming at perfection, and the real thing; and mark me, you haven't got very much further to go.

George.

My first theatrical engagement after leaving the ESA was as understudy to Bernard Lee and Assistant Stage Manager at the Savoy Theatre in a play called *Night Sky* by L. Du Garde Peach. This was January 1937 and my salary was £2 10s per week. The play was about the next war, which we didn't take very seriously but L. Du Garde Peach did. It was full of searchlights and brave pilots and was fairly prophetic but I suppose it wasn't very entertaining as it only ran for ten performances. People didn't want to know about war and it was not a subject which drew them into the Savoy.

Osmond Daltry, the young man I had met during amdram days at Stevenage, had got together with a rich stage-struck Australian lady who had put her money into theatrical management. They were running a company called Westminster Productions. She offered me my first decent role in a professional company, which was playing Lodovico in *Othello* at the People's Palace Theatre, Mile End Road, in 1937. Stephen Murray played Othello and later I was paid £1 a week extra to understudy him, in addition to understudying the Duke of Venice. I have proudly kept the contract.

Another moving spirit behind this artistic venture, Pat Ide, was a lovely man now alas no more, and I am eternally grateful to Osmond Daltry for introducing me to him. He was a great inspiration, full of help, encouragement and wit. When the two-week run of *Othello* was over he invited me to audition for a tour he was arranging, taking three English plays to the main cities of Scandinavia and the Baltic. It was the only audition in which I have been successful and I secured the parts of Henry in *Outward Bound* and Sergius in *Arms and the Man*. My professional acting career had begun.

The tour was great fun and I adored it. We were a very happy company, the plays went well and, as we each had one play out, we were able to combine pleasure with business and have a good look around the places we visited. I thought 'this is for me', but after the glories of Scandinavia I eventually found myself in London with no work. However, the management of the Savoy were about to present *Ninety Sail*, a play about Christopher Wren and the English Navy. As it was simply crammed with parts I was assured of work in three weeks' time when rehearsals were to begin. So I counted the money I had in the bank, which came to £30, and went to Poland, chasing a lady.

Wanda Zielinska was a beautiful Polish girl I had met at a dance in England a year or two previously. We got to know each other very well. We never became lovers, although I was very attracted to her and she to me. She was great fun and danced beautifully—so did I in those days, when you held your partner and didn't jiggle about with your fists in the air.

I took off for Warsaw with a third-class railway ticket and booked into the Europeski Hotel. It was the time of a religious

DATE *February 16th* 195 7.

Dear *Mr Michael Horden*

    Will you please accept this letter as a contract form
between us regarding our production of " ~~gun AND THE MOON~~ "OTHELLO"",
at the People's Palace, Mile End Road, E.
You are required to attend rehearsals as required and to play
for two weeks, nightly at 8.p.m. from Monday the 8th, of Febuary,
with two matinees on Thursday the 11th, and 18th, respectively.
For this engagement your salary will be. *£ 4.10*..........
as agreed plus *£ 2 -0-0*........ rehearsal expenses.
Please sign and return the enclosed duplicate.

               Yours sincerely,
          p.p.Westminster Productions Ltd.

                DIRECTOR.

The Part of *Lodovico*...
& understudy Duke of Venice.

festival in Poland, with much feasting and dancing. Wanda and I danced every night somewhere or other. Warsaw was full of Polish army officers in their uniforms and there was much gold braid and clicking heels. There were all sorts of dances which I didn't know but soon learnt. It was great fun. We were driven about in drotskis in the snow, romantically holding hands under the fur rugs. Then we went back to bed, she to her parents' flat overlooking the Vistula, and I to my hotel. It was all very proper.

Not long after this, those glorious Polish officers were to be massacred at Katyn. Wanda was in England when the war broke out and her parents telegraphed her to come back home immediately. She went straight home into the thick of it.

I had had this marvellous fortnight in Warsaw, spent all my money and had a few Zlotys left, which I was under the mistaken impression were worth about £9 or £10. I had got the exchange rate muddled and in fact had about ten pence to see me through this long third-class journey back to England, with a five-hour wait in Berlin. I was carrying with me a pineapple and a huge box of beautiful chocolates as a present from my Polish hosts to friends in London. By the end of the journey both the chocolates and the pineapple had been consumed but I was feeling quite cheerful with the prospect of almost immediate employment. However, when I reported to the Savoy Theatre I discovered that the play had been cancelled. So there I was in my little digs at Marble Arch, without a penny in the world, having sold my soul to the devil, as it were. I often wonder how I existed. Perhaps kind Mr Thorsby, the snack-bar man, took pity on me and gave me credit. Anyway, Patrick Ide came to my rescue again and introduced me to his great friend Ronald Russell, who ran a weekly repertory company: The Rapier Players, at the Colston Hall, Bristol. I went to Bristol, was interviewed by Ronald Russell, and got the job.

The Little Theatre in Bristol had been formally opened on 17 December 1923 by Sir Arthur Wing Pinero with these words:

. . . I beg to be allowed to congratulate you on having achieved the beginning of a repertory theatre and upon the character of the scheme we are present to inaugurate. When Sir Robert Harvey wrote to me about the scheme, he said that the initial season of Bristol's Little Theatre is to be run on common-sense lines. I rejoice to hear that, because the word common-sense conveys to my mind the assurance that the repertory theatre is not to be exclusively highbrow. Since I have had an opportunity of reading the full programme of the season, I am glad to find that my interpretation of Mr Harvey's letter is correct. I should be sorry to be suspected of a desire to lessen the importance of having plays that are called highbrow, for I have done a little in that line myself. But I do venture to say that a repertory theatre that is given up to plays of that description places a limit on the range of its appeal and narrows the sphere of usefulness. I would go further and say that I am glad they are to give plays that could not be regarded as highbrow, but that are worthy of the attention and respect of intelligent audiences . . .

Six years later, Ronnie Russell, fresh from Clifton College, started work at the Little Theatre, Bristol, as a student assistant, his first job being to light the gas heater and deliver hot water to the dressing rooms. He graduated to assistant stage manager, and having left to gain experience in other theatres, returned in 1935 as producer. It was this same Ronnie Russell to whom Patrick Ide introduced me in 1937 and it was he who was to turn me into a professional actor.

Ronnie Russell ran The Little Theatre Company for twenty-eight years, and gave it the thrusting, go-ahead name of the Rapier Players. Even during the war, Ronnie and his wife, the actress Peggy Ann Wood, refused to be defeated by Hitler: while Ronnie joined the police force, Peggy Ann took the company on the road, touring around the countryside for the whole of the war, eventually returning home to a packed Little Theatre on Good Friday 1941, the day after the last blitz.

Anything to do with the theatre is never easy. I understand absolutely nothing about running a theatre nowadays and I certainly had no thought of it then. I was talking to Ronnie Russell last year over lunch in the flat in Bristol where he and Peggy Ann still live, and he vividly recalled some of the problems of making ends meet in an unsubsidised repertory theatre in the 1940s. 'We had a "get out" figure of £250 a week to cover everything; rent, rates, salaries, upkeep, etc. In a good week we did £200–£250 on the door, seat prices being 3/6d, 2/6d or 1/-, and thirty seats at the door at 1/-. From programme sales and café profits we made £30, so we just about managed. I was director and administrator and my salary was £7 plus 2 percent of box office takings. If we had a good week, I would get £12, so I wasn't exactly raking it in.'

Our stage manager was Albert Malpas, the carpenter, who did everything: set changes, lighting, get ins, get outs, and he even swept the dressing rooms. There was an enormous amount for Albert to do, especially as all the flats had to be brought up from the basement. He was also the most marvellous prompter. Prompting well is a real craft, which too few stage managers understand. As well as concentration and clarity, it requires tact and intuition. Albert was brilliant at this and could often mime a word so you could catch the meaning and get back on the rails.

We had nothing as sophisticated as a designer, but there

were a lot of interchangeable flats which were kept in stock and repainted about every nine months when they became too cracked. There was the oak set, the red set, the yellow set and two or three cloths, one of which Albert called 'the gentleman's garden' because it had pillars, and another, more fancifully, 'country hedgerow'.

Ronnie eventually put an advertisement in the local paper for a commissionaire and, fresh out of school, two good-looking boys called Bright and Upton appeared. We never knew which was Bright and which was Upton, as they were always together. They weren't gay. In fact, when they first saw a particularly beautiful actress in the company called Valerie White, they nearly fell into the footlights with excitement. They were very strong and must have made a huge difference to Albert's life. One would dress in a commissionaire's uniform and go out front to sell tickets and, as soon as the house was in, change into dungarees and join the others moving flats backstage. Such was weekly rep in 1940.

So it was I found myself a member of the Rapier Players in Bristol, being paid £5 a week. I started the 1937 season playing a character called Uncle Henry in a play the title of which escapes me, feeling very disappointed at having to play an old uncle. Thereafter I played old uncles and faithful retainers for weeks and weeks. Having recently seen Gerald du Maurier at Wyndham's Theatre, in London and much admired him and his stylish way with a silver cigarette case, I was convinced that there was a leading man in me wanting to get out. But I was not allowed, for what seemed like a lifetime, to play the leading man; and quite right too!

On the first day of rehearsal I was to meet the two juvenile actresses. One was a very pretty blonde, Margaret Fry, and the other a lovely brunette, Eve Mortimer, who, years later, was to become my wife.

In weekly rep you had to provide all your own modern

clothes. We were given a great list of things that were considered absolutely essential. Men had to find a blazer, grey flannels, a lounge suit, dinner jacket, and I think, tails. The girls had to have, amongst other things, a cocktail dress and something called 'matching accessories'. It was much more difficult for them as they couldn't be seen in the same outfit twice. So much ingenuity was called for and there was a great deal of borrowing and running things up on a sewing machine. Some actresses became so adept at this that patrons often used to come to the theatre each week, as much as anything to see the actresses' latest outfit. Oh, the great relief when we were doing a costume play and the hamper would come down from Berman's or Morris Angel; there would be an unseemly scuffle to get the best costume and find the right wig.

Rehearsals were very perfectly timed. You were allowed two minutes a page, so, if you didn't come in until page twenty you knew exactly what time to arrive at rehearsal. Time was at a premium in weekly rep. There was no time for analysis or any deep psychological investigation into a part. It really was a question, as Noel Coward said, of 'learn the lines and don't bump into the furniture'. It certainly meant you had no time to worry whether something was right. You just had to do it and see.

Ronnie Russell was marvellous at knowing exactly how much direction he could give in a week. I have worked with directors since who overdirect some parts of a play, so that others are never rehearsed at all! Ronnie knew exactly how much time he could spend on such and such a scene and give the best time at his disposal—two minutes a page. He taught me what it was all about. I owe him and Patrick Ide more than anybody else I have ever met in my professional life.

There could be no more dreary entertainment in England than the midweek matinée at Bristol's Little Theatre. Nevertheless, Conrad Fry (of the chocolate-makers) and his male secretary would be there every Wednesday. There they would be, whatever the play, always in the same seats and surrounded by old ladies. At least it wasn't a tea matinée. I have, thankfully, never done one. There is a story about Henry Ainley playing Hamlet at a tea matinée and being driven mad by the sound of clinking cups and slurping. Being unable to get on with it, he shouted '*To be or not to be that is the* TEA. Whether tis nobler in the mind to suffer the slings and arrows of outrageous TEA . . .' I wonder if they took the hint and shut up.

At the end of our first season in Bristol, Eve and I set off for a holiday in Scotland in an old Riley Nine that I was buying for £60 on hire purchase. The car wasn't going very well. I didn't know anything about cars then and I still don't know anything now: all I can do is open the bonnet and cry. I just hoped it would cheer up, and, to our astonishment, it did. We spent that first night at Pitlochry and then a marvellous three days down the Tay at Daiham Bridge, where we were lent about a mile of fishing and a ready-made camp pitched already for us by one Charley Briton. We were allowed to catch what we liked. The salmon weren't there, the peel weren't taking and we didn't get many trout but it was such a heavenly spot and the nights down by the riverbank and the smell of the frying fish for breakfast will never be forgotten. According to my 1935 fishing diary:

Rain, rain, rain. Some very nice people Mr and Mrs Pitt of Boxmoor who came last night for a week, took me down to the Orkey and we salmon fished the river rising and rising not a fish to be seen. We lunched off whiskey, went down to look at the falls which were magnificently in spate and came home to a hot bath and more whiskey.

We've been sitting in the hotel ever since. The rain stopped at about 7.30 after being at it for about 24 hours and by night the loch stretches about 500 yds further west up the glen than it should and the trees peeping out of the face of the waters make me feel like Noah, though the inn makes a comfortable ark with not too many animals! The sides of the mountains are streaked with falling water and where the burns enter the loch tongues of white foam flow out into the middle over the black water. The Pitts are a most awfully good couple and we three now feel quite possessive about the pub. The Orkey of course will be quite out of order tomorrow but I wonder if there will be trout to be caught among the hay-cocks over what was yesterdays meadow by the side of Loch Tulla.

The river appeared to be in top hole condition and the pool lousy with fish. None of us rose a thing and apart from falling in the river there is nothing to write. Two good 'mots' though. Scots fisherman off for a week-end in his smack tells his boy to go and get his provisions. Boy returns with 24 bottles of whiskey and a loaf of bread, 'Och,' says the fisherman, 'and what's all the bread for?' And again, the Pitts' ghillie at Durness, where they have just been, to Mrs P who was explaining to him how she was inclined to be fairly talkative, 'Och,' says he, 'but it's a good thing, a silent woman's like a rocky pool!' This ghillie, Angus, is also responsible for the description of bad casting, which has become a byword this last week—'casting like a "hane" (hen),' he said. In the evening the pub was very full and we did the *Times* crossword and felt comatose.

We camped, or stayed in little pubs, and had a wonderful holiday, meeting up with some old friends of mine, the

Dyballs, and fishing with them in the northwest of Scotland. Leslie Dyball landed a 19 lb salmon on a trout rod in the little River Dionard, which was something of a record. I tried to teach Eve to fish: it was rather like teaching your nearest and dearest to drive—in other words, hopeless. She did a little just to keep me company, but it never really grabbed her.

As I had a part in a radio play back in Bristol, I had to be there before the beginning of the theatre season. Dropping Eve off at Liverpool to see her family, I drove south to keep my appointment with the BBC. I had an almighty smash *en route*, very nearly killing the lady driver in the other car. Fortunately, the lady eventually made a full recovery, but that was the end of my car. I had only paid one instalment: there were eleven more to go and the Riley was a total write-off. So it was that I turned up at the BBC to do my first radio play, carrying a sack full of fishing tackle and a primus stove. The play was *Quinneys*, starring Henry Ainley, a great actor who, sadly, was by then past his best.

I was happily placed as my father had sold Jordan Manor and bought a house in Holt, a little village not far from Bristol. So I dossed down there for the rest of the summer break. I wasn't destitute. Then back to my 'digs' with the Miss Emms for the beginning of my second Bristol season, which opened with Stella Gibbons' *Cold Comfort Farm*.

Cold Comfort Farm horrified Bristol audiences, who imagined they would be in for an evening of pastoral idyll. Instead they were treated to a complete send-up of all pastoral idylls and they left in droves. We all adored it as a company. It was enormous fun to play all those outrageous parts. I played Seth, whose shirt buttons were always undone. Mrs Starkadder was played by a well-known radio actress, Mabel Constanduros, who had adapted the book.

In the summer of 1939, Eve and I both left Bristol after two very happy years. Eve joined the White Rose Players in

Harrogate and I was fancy-free. I was staying with my friends the Dyballs in Hertfordshire when war broke out. Everything stopped, the theatres closed and we all expected to be bombed at any moment. I was very much in love with Eve and my first thought was to get up to Harrogate to be with her. We decided we would go back to Bristol to die with our friends. I remember, when we were catching the train from Leeds, seeing a young soldier in tears, saying goodbye to his girlfriend at the station. In fear and trembling we took the train to Bristol, expecting to be bombed every time the train stopped. We thought 'This must be it'. It was the phoney war. The first bombs were not to fall for six months.

CHAPTER 4

Joining the Navy

As there was no work in Bristol, I volunteered for Heavy Rescue in the ARP Air Raid Precautions. This meant standing by, to leap at a moment's notice, into the heavy rescue waggons and go to dig people out of bombed buildings. As there were no bombs, there was no digging to be done—in fact, nothing to be done at all. This didn't seem to me to be a very good way to fight the war, so I volunteered for the Navy.

I decided on the Navy as I had painful memories of army cadet days at school; I couldn't bear the thought of scratchy khaki uniform and seeing the whites of the enemy's eyes. I wasn't very brave but I preferred the look of those bellbottom trousers. Their Lordships, not having much immediate need for my services, suggested I go back and follow my chosen profession, whatever that might be, and they would let me know if they needed me.

The theatres were starting to open again and, not much wanting to go back into heavy rescue, I answered, with Eve, an advertisement in *The Stage* for actors to audition for a new repertory company being formed in The Assembly Rooms, Bath. We were to be interviewed by one Eveline Purkiss, who gave us to understand that we would be amazed by 'the names' who had answered her advertisement. Intimidated by this news, we naturally didn't expect even small parts in a company where such famous actors were queuing up to work with Eveline Purkiss. To our great joy and delight, however, we were engaged and, arriving for our first rehearsal, found we were the leading man and leading lady!

We took digs together in Bath. I was expecting to be called up at any moment; in fact, I was called up just before the 1939 Christmas show. As I was playing the leading part, this made things very awkward. I pointed this out to the Navy, who were very understanding, saying they would try to manage without me until after the Christmas show. So, after the last performance, in the year 1940, I packed away my greasepaint and reported for duty. 'I'm ready now, let battle commence,' I said to myself as I donned my bellbottoms. I went down to train at Plymouth Barracks.

This was a joining routine consisting of weeks of square-bashing, bends and hitches. Here, one day on the parade ground, quite low down, popping in and out of the clouds above our heads, I saw the enemy for the first time, a German plane on reconnaissance. The French having just surrendered, quite a few big ships from their fleet had nipped across the Channel and sought asylum in Plymouth.

I volunteered to be a DEMS gunner. DEMS stands for Defensively Equipped Merchant Ship. All merchant ships carried defensive armament manned by naval ratings. We took a three-week course in Cardiff, many of my contemporaries being Welsh miners, splendid people, and we got on very well indeed. In the fullness of time, I passed the fairly primitive gunnery course, but the first time I pulled the trigger I got an awful shock—I didn't care for the noise.

I was sent to an old merchant ship, the *City of Florence*. She was a 7000-ton, two-deck, steel-hulled cargo ship built in 1918 and, to my horror, she was being loaded with projectiles and ammunition to be taken out to Alexandria for the British fleet.

A very senior gunner with me was Corporal Young, a pensioner of the Royal Marines, a tiny, 'pukka' little man who stood to attention all the time and called me 'Lofty' because I was so tall. He hated my guts. He was in his fifties, had been brought back for the war and was forever polishing the brass on his uniform. He was rather a nice chap really, but he couldn't bear me or the class from which he considered I came.

Britain was very much more class-conscious in those days than it is today and Corporal Young found himself caught between two classes. As a fighting man, he was superior to the merchant navy crew and found himself mixing with its officer class. Although I was junior to him on the gun and just an acting able seaman who didn't know anything about the sea, I was of the officer class. This was all very confusing and frustrating to an experienced Royal Marine who loved the sea and was happy to find himself in uniform again.

We shared a cabin in our little deck house—my bunk on the port side, his on the starboard side—and he completely ignored me. This went on for ten months and was an awful strain. The only time he spoke to me was to give orders on the gun or occasionally when we got drunk together. Then everything would change and we became the best of friends, talking our heads off about life, love, politics, arts, sex, class distinction and much else. But as soon as we were sober again the barriers went up and absolute silence descended. We were like two different people. I think he had a wife somewhere but he never mentioned her.

The war was hotting up, and there were air raids in Newport. We didn't like air raids at all, sitting as we were on top of all this ammunition. Then we had a fire. Returning from a shore visit, I found the ship being unloaded of its cargo of shells and fearsome weaponry. 'Oh how lovely,' I thought. 'Perhaps they will fill us with nice things like timber and salt.' But no. Once the cause of the fire was discovered, all the explosives were put back and we became a sailing minefield again, off to join a convoy of half a dozen ships from the Bristol Channel, then up the Irish Sea to pick up an even bigger convoy off Glasgow and out into the Atlantic.

At sea on the second night we were attacked by a 'wolf pack' of U-boats. This was the real thing: no film stars in a tank at Pinewood Studios but proud ships and the reality of men trying to be brave. The five ships nearest to us went down in five minutes. It was terrifying. The Corporal and I and the gun crews we had trained, who were all Indians and Lascars and not awfully good at gunnery, manned the guns. We tried to be brave and train the guns on where we thought the action was but we couldn't see a thing. The night passed with the ships in the convoy hooting to each other and trampling on each other's backsides trying to get out of the way. We stood down at daybreak and were alone. There was not another ship in sight. What was left of the convoy had either dispersed or been sunk. I was frightened that night, the second night out and almost my last. That was when I grew up. A shell had been left in the gun from the night's work but, as the captain was afraid of detection, we were forced to continue course for Durban with a shell up the spout. We managed to conceal from the Durban authorities that the gun was loaded and it wasn't until we sailed into the Indian Ocean that we were finally allowed to fire it. The long lanyard was pulled, the gun went off and the sternpost fell out of the ship. Eventually, arriving in Alexandria, we thankfully delivered our dangerous cargo.

It was the time of Field Marshal Wavell's first push in North Africa and the British Army were taking Italian prisoners, not by the hundred but by the thousand. The *City of Florence* and any other empty vessels in the vicinity were commanded by the authorities to sail along the North African coast and pick up as many of these Italian prisoners as they could. The *Florence* was only an old 7000-ton merchant ship, but we picked up literally hundreds of these prisoners from Sollum. They came out to us in lighters during the day and were loaded into the ship. We couldn't stay in Sollum harbour overnight and risk being bombed so in the evening, to avoid being a sitting target, we sailed out into the Mediterranean and steamed around all night. We would repeat this performance the next day, filling up with more prisoners until we had as many as we could hold. Then we took them to Alexandria. Many of the prisoners were only too delighted to escape the war but conditions were rugged; they were squashed in the hold and only periodically allowed up on deck in groups to get some fresh air.

They longed for cigarettes and, as we could get these cheaply, the Corporal and I bought tins of Woodbines, cut the cigarettes in half and distributed them amongst the clamoring prisoners. In return they pressed us to take the pictures of the saints from their prayerbooks. They were a friendly bunch and there was no trouble, which was remarkable given the appalling conditions. Luckily it was only a short trip from Sollum to Alexandria, where they were put ashore and sent off to prison camps. Having safely transported the last prisoner, the old *City of Florence* was returned to its shipping company, the City Line.

Our first trip was to Colombo and then across the Indian Ocean to Rangoon 'on the road to Mandalay, where the flying fishes play'. There was a desperate gaiety about our runs ashore.

Rangoon was wonderful. I was lucky enough to be able to go and stay with some friends of friends who treated me like a king. They were very much the last of the British Raj, enjoying a very unwarlike lifestyle with beautiful food, tennis parties and servants padding about opening curtains and bringing early morning tea in a silver pot. With war raging round the rest of the world, it felt rather immoral but oh the relief of it all. It was a fascinating time; I did nothing very gay and exciting but enjoyed wandering about, getting the smell of Burma, seeing the Schwedagon Pagoda and going to the cathedral where my parents had been married and find their signatures in the register. After two indulgent weeks, it was back to the bellbottom trousers and on board the dirty old *City of Florence*. Loaded up with fresh, and this time less dangerous, cargo we set off homewards, looking for the shark that never came.

It was not long after this that the Japanese joined the war and my friends' scented lifestyle changed. Tracking through the jungle, they had a terrible time getting out of Burma, and they had to leave their beautiful things behind, but they survived.

I had this enormous hook under my bunk. It had taken me time and trouble to forge lovingly out of a butcher's meat hook and it had a length of sounding wire attached, what a fly fisherman might call a 'leader'. There it was, waiting for sharks. They didn't seem to come to the ports at which we called, but then one day . . .

The *City of Florence* not being the newest vessel that ever plied the seas, we were always breaking down. One Sunday in the Indian Ocean, homeward bound between Rangoon and Durban, the engines came to a cranking stop. It was midday and equatorially hot. I was sunning myself in a deckchair when a shout went up: 'Michael, a shark, a shark!' I ran to the rail and saw a shark nosing up against the ship. Dashing back to my bunk and picking up my beautiful hook, which had been ready for six months, I called in at the galley for a chunk of raw meat. Impaling it on the hook, I ran up on deck and chucked it at the shark, the crew leaning over the rail to cheer and give advice. The shark abandoned his exploration, turned on his back and took the bait like a trout taking a mayfly. I heaved on my primitive tackle but he turned over again, spat the bait back and disappeared. A shout from the other side of the ship told me the shark had either gone round or underneath and had popped up on the starboard side. Again I threw the hook and bait, and this time he took it properly. Turning my back until I judged the bait taken, I gave the line a heave and battle was joined. There was an almighty tussle as the shark thrashed about wildly and I grimly remained connected to the other end, playing it, so to speak. The trouble in the engine room now repaired, the captain wanted to get under way but sportingly gave me five minutes to get the shark aboard. One of the brave Indian crew, going down the ladder over the side, managed to get a noose round the creature's tail and we heaved it aboard. The crew descended upon it, bashing it over the head and then, as happens in the best sailing-ship stories, slitting it open to see if there were any gold rings and treasure in the guts. Alas—nothing. I extracted the rows of terrifying teeth with the idea that they would make a necklace for Eve, but the smell, weeks later, when they were handed over to their recipient in England, was awful. Eve was less than thrilled. I took the backbone out and pegged it on top of the deck-house to cure it in the sun, thinking to make of it a splendid walking stick, but that didn't materialise either and we didn't eat it so the poor shark came to a useless end.

After this wonderfully peaceful trip across the Indian Ocean we picked up the convoy at Durban to come home. As this was a silent convoy, not allowed radio communication, we had to signal by semaphore and Aldis lamps. Very slowly, terribly slowly, at the speed of the slowest ship, this huge convoy came zig-zagging back to Britain. It was extraordinary to look out at first light and see this mass of ships on station—forty or fifty of them with an escort of cruisers—apparently stationary just as they had been at last light the night before. There seemed to be absolutely no onward movement. We appeared 'as idle as a painted ship upon a painted ocean' and then suddenly the whole angle of the convoy would change.

We played a lot of bridge on the *City of Florence*, the skipper, the chief engineer, one or two of the ship's officers and myself. I got on very well with the four English quartermasters, all of them extraordinarily different characters, who took the wheel and kept watch. Living on deck in a sort of hutch was a dour Scot who came from the Outer Hebrides, a wild unshaven man called Bill and a teenager who was very frightened of the sea. Then there was a much older man who was like a ghost in the background and quite silent. I got on well with them too. How good people were! I didn't appreciate at the time how difficult it must have been for them to accept me as well as they did when I knew nothing about the sea, only about the gun I was there to aim. It was a strange year. I was absolutely out of my range and out of my class. I had led a very sheltered middle-class life at Jordan and public school. To be pitched into living intimately with people whose outlook and experience of life was so different from mine was undoubtedly very good for me. I knew nothing about their life and yet they accepted me.

The great silent convoy bore up around the British Isles and we went round the top, 'northabout' to London. Coming ashore at Tilbury, I reported to Naval Command, who seemed to be of the opinion that I should take a commission. Although I had proudly worn my naval uniform for the best part of a year, I had no real understanding of anything nautical and when asked by an officer to 'box the compass' I hadn't the faintest idea what he meant. Despite this deficiency I was judged to be if not an 'instant officer' then officer material and sent down to

Brighton where an officer training establishment had been set up in the King Alfred Baths. Here I learnt the mysteries of compass boxing and spent a good deal of time crunching all night on Brighton beach doing sentry duty. Then I went on to Lancing College, where we were 'polished off' and turned into officers and, sometimes, gentlemen. We learnt how to sit in front of a desk and how to navigate an old naval tender around Newhaven, giving the right orders to the wheel. Amazingly, I passed out top of my division. They must have been a rum lot!

About this time, radar was coming into service in the Navy. The technicalities of radar baffled me and watching the scan and pressing buttons confused me greatly but the information received was invaluable. The ranges and bearing were used for targeting, gunnery, submarines and torpedoes, and for directing aircraft. It was suggested that this would be excellent work for me with my strong actor's voice and so I was one of the first naval officers to be trained in the use of radar for directing fighter aircraft. We had three weeks' training at Yeovilton Air Station, where we learnt the rudiments of radar, talking on the radio telephone in plain language to the pilots and giving them courses to intercept the enemy. So in the spring of 1942, after this intense training, I was posted as Fighter Direction Officer to one of the greatest ships in the British Navy, a ship in which I was to serve for the next two and a half years, HMS *Illustrious*.

Anybody who knows anything about the British Navy over the last fifty years knows about *Illustrious*. She was a great aircraft carrier and a magnificent ship not dissimilar in appearance from the new National Theatre building. Because of someone's misplaced faith in me, I was lucky enough to find myself serving on this great ship, second in command to a very good chap called David Pollock who was an RNR two and a half, a lieutenant-commander. Unfortunately, he was not to be on board for very long. After sailing out of Liverpool and carrying out an operation on Madagascar, he was transferred to a desk job at the Admiralty and I was left as the only trained Fighter Direction Officer in the British fleet. My rank was upped immediately to lieutenant-commander and there I stayed for another two years serving under three or four captains and several admirals.

'What were you in peacetime, Hordern?'
'An actor, Sir.'
'Right, you're in charge of entertainments.'

Captain Arthur George Talbot was Captain when I joined *Illustrious* and he had a terrible reputation as a bully boy. Fortunately, he soon moved on to higher things, but not before he had detailed me as officer in charge of entertainments. I am useless at delegating, absolutely no producer or director, but found myself in charge of the entertainments on this vast ship of over two thousand souls. Though I felt daunted by the whole thing, I nevertheless began to appreciate that an aircraft carrier is a jolly good ship on which to have any kind of theatrical entertainment. There was an enormous space under the flight deck and the huge aircraft lifts when raised, made a splendid stage. There was a lot of real talent around. *Illustrious* carried the Royal Marines Band and, with the bandmaster conducting from the splendid orchestra pit we had constructed, they made a splendid noise that raised everyone's spirits. We were lucky enough to have aboard Robert Eddison, a witty man with a lively imagination, and a very good actor who featured with me in several sketches full of terrible jokes and badinage much appreciated by the ratings. This is the pro-gramme for a concert we gave aboard HMS *Illustrious* in about 1942, when I was Entertainments Officer.

1   THE ROYAL MARINE BAND PLAYS.
2   STANLEY PAYTON will impersonate various people
3   JIM INGRAM and his piano accordion
4   BOOSALOT Mr Boosalot—Jimmie Currie
                 Ccl. Fitzlollipop—Treveleyan Roberts
                 Lady Ruff-Orpington—Harry Mann
                 Mr Taboosh—Arthur Probert
5   Bert Mathews will sing
6   Go to Hell 1st sailor—Leslie Hunter
                 2nd sailor—Michael Hordern
7   George McCabe in Illuminated Clubs
8   Baron Chiselovski and his Oil Fuel
                 Manipulators Orchestra

INTERVAL

9   Arthur Probert our Lancashire Comic
10 SEA-SCAPE Mavis—Robert Eddison
                 Lorelei—Michael Hordern
11 JIM HARFORD and TOMMY LORD playing on
        their trumpets.
12 A LADY SINGS —Michael Hordern
13 ROBERT EVERETT at the Pictures
14 EASTERN ROMANCE Sheik—Harry Mann
                 Shake Charmer—Clifford Wallis
                 Miss Flower—E. F. Brayley and
                         Jessie Mathews, Raymond Ingledew
                         Nicholas Carter, Daisy Bell
                         Gut Smith, Duncan Lougdon
15 Landing on.
        The Captain—Alec Foulerton
        The O. O. W.—Arthur Johnson

The Navigator—Roger Fisher
16   THE FINALE sung by Ronald Berry
      COMPERE ROBERT EDDISON, THE KING

★★★★★

Directed by Michael Hordern
Musical Director Leonard C. Bagley
STAGE DIRECTOR Charles Croucher
STAGE MANAGER Leslie Hunter
LIGHTING by TORPS ELECTRIC
Cigarettes by pusser
Gowns by all sorts of people

Especially popular was the sketch called *Sea-Scape*, which featured Robert and myself being particularly seductive as mermaids, Mavis and Lorelei, wearing beautiful tails and exchanging pleasantries as we sat on the anchor of *Illustrious* at the bottom of the sea. On tattered, battered Navy war-issue paper I found this fragile copy of the masterpiece of which Robert and I were so proud and which had our fellow seamates crying for more. Difficult reading it now to understand why it was such a riot—must have been our brilliant delivery.

SEA-SCAPE

The scene is, in short, the bottom of the Ocean. Whatever may be done to suggest this should be done, the basic minimum being an elegant scallop shell of some size (sufficiently large, in fact, to contain a Mermaid: it is her home) which is at the moment closed. Seated on an eminence of some kind is another Mermaid. She is no longer young and is, perhaps, giving more attention to her toilette than is strictly justified. She is combing her rather dishevelled hair, gazing into a mirror, and singing at her reflection with a certain distaste. Her name is Mavis.

Mavis: Mirror, Mirror, tell me truly
Who is the fairest lady in the land?
She comes to a tough lock.
Damn my bloddy hair, it's most unruly;
And if there's one thing worse than scurf . . . it's sand.
A telephone bell rings. Mavis evinces no surprise and reaches down behind her, producing from thereabouts a telephone.

Hullo? Oh, hullo Leonora . . . Lorelei? No dear, she isn't up yet . . . no dear: plastered! . . . She broached that barrel of Rum last night that came down with the Hesperus . . . *you* remember . . . yes dear, that's the one; the Skipper who was such a bore about his little daughter . . . quite, dear, quite: I'm only quoting them . . . I know dear, but that's what they always *said*, that she was his daughter . . . you're telling me! . . . A dirty old man? My dear, I'm perfectly certain he was a *filthy* old man; and mind you, *we* didn't see him at his worst, all limp and bedraggled like that after his ducking . . . don't be disgusting dear: I didn't mean anything like that! . . . Well dear, I'll knock on her Conch if you like: she may be awake by now.

She gives a sharp rap on the shell by her side, but there is no response

No dear, no response . . . don't be unkind dear; she hadn't been on a bender for weeks, and it *was* rather an occasion . . . well dear, in her condition . . . Oh! my dear! Hadn't you heard? . . . Yes my dear, yesterday, in the Last Dog . . . spawned all over the place: at her age

71

too . . . darling there hasn't been such a hysterical triumph since the relief of Ladysmith . . . oh, I don't know dear, some old Victorian trout . . . What? . . . Oh well, my dear, we don't quite *know*, but I have my suspicions . . . Well, I can only say that she came back all girlish from that 'do' at the 'Snorting Grampus' on Fishmas Eve.

Ned Silver got his nickname . . . Don't be silly, dear, of course *we* knew . . . the thing's been sticking out a mile for years . . . but Lorelei is still very innocent in some ways . . No dear, not conclusive I admit, but you can't help putting one and one together . . . Yes, allright . . . yes, I'll tell her. You *must* swim over to lunch one day . . . Yes, we'll settle a date later. Bye-bye, ducks.

> The shell is creeping open now, and a very jaded figure is observed. This is Lorelei, also past her first youth, but more determined to conceal the fact, which she attempts to do by various Little-Womanly affectations.

Good morning, Little Mother.

Lorelei: Don't *shout*, Mavis dear; don't be so *noisy*! And there's no need to be facetious either. Motherhood is a very beautiful thing.

Mavis: Yes I know dear: that girl from the Mexican Gulf was saying only the other day that you looked 'swell'.

Lorelei: Oh how can you be so heartless! I've had a very trying time.

Mavis: And my dear, how brilliantly you succeeded! It's the buzz of the Doldrums! Oh, by the way, there's a telegram for you.

Lorelei: Who's it from?

Mavis: I don't know. I popped it under the milk so that it shouldn't float away.

Lorelei: Oh yes, the milk! Thank God I shan't need any more of that building-up nonsense . . . remind me to stop it: even now I weigh more than I ought to. Oh *dear* what I've been through! Open it for me, there's a dear. And those *awful* Maternity shells I had to wear made me look twice as big as I needed to. I suppose *every-*one guessed, though I think I was pretty cunning on the whole. Well, who's it from? What's it say?

Mavis: 'Well done, darling! We all knew you had it in you.' It's unsigned.

Lorelei: *Oh*! I know: it's that *bitch*-fish Jacqueline; she was always jealous about it. How *petty*! Oh well, never mind . . . Open the milk for me darling: I think I'll have it after all . . . my mouth's like the bottom of a Lobster Pot.

Mavis: Leonora rang up, by the way.

Lorelei: Oh? What did she want?

Mavis: Nothing I don't think.

My party piece—which went under the title *A Lady Sings* and which I half sung, half spoke—was an innocent enough little nursery rhyme that, for some reasons, had the ratings and officers alike falling in the aisles.

I've got a little pussy. It's so pretty and so small.
I'm sure it's quite the nicest little pussy cat of all.
Some people say they like a pussy very large and fine
But when they do I say to them oh! you should just see mine.

My little pussy is prettier than yours,
Nice long whiskers, never shows its claws.
I never give it meat, because I want to keep it small.
My little pussy is the prettiest of all.

73

Some people like a tabby or a Persian with long hair
But for that kind of pussy I'm quite sure I wouldn't care.
While others like a black one or a white one I've heard tell
But mine's a perfect beauty, it's a lovely tortoiseshell.

My little pussy is prettier than yours, . . . etc

The curate often calls and of my pussy makes a fuss
He loves to stroke and play with it, he is so fond of us
His wife has got a pussy which he often has caressed
He says although it's very nice, he likes my pussy best.

My little pussy is prettier than yours, etc

The whole thing was directed by Malcolm Baker Smith, who later became one of the first television directors and was to give me my first television part after the war. Malcolm was working for the Admiralty and came on board to write a television programme about aircraft carriers. Although we didn't know it, we were getting ready to go to Madagascar and the captain drew Malcolm to one side, suggesting that, although he ought by rights to be leaving the ship, if he hid for a while he might wake up to find himself on the way to action in the Indian Ocean. This he did and stayed with us for some months, shooting loads of valuable film and being a great help with the entertainments. We also rigged up a studio in the bowels of the ship where I practised being a disc jockey and played record requests, which inevitably included Vera Lynn and *Blue Birds over the White Cliffs of Dover*.

One could see why *Illustrious* had come to be known as the 'happiest floating hotel in the southern hemisphere' and sometimes as 'the only floating lunatic asylum run by its own inmates'. Apart from a short time under Arthur George, she was indeed a very happy ship. Captain Bob 'Smiler' Cunliffe, who followed Arthur George, could not have been more different. He liked the men and sought their company. Together with Commander Arthur Wallis and Rear-Admiral 'Clem' Moody, he seemed to know the Christian names and nicknames of all the men and contributed hugely to the very happy atmosphere on board.

At some point Admiral Mountbatten had been captain of *Illustrious*. I had met him in Colombo when he was Commander-in-Chief of the Eastern Fleet. He came on board, inspected us and came round to my Fighter Direction position, where I delivered him a short lecture on the mysteries of telephone communications. He must have been very properly impressed as none of the high-ranking officers knew anything about it. He was a handsome figure of a man, standing there in his tropical gear, but I thought he had suspicious hips.

One of the perks of my unexpected promotion to lieutenant-commander was a very grand cabin which, although extremely comfortable and luxurious, was very dull, so I had it cheered up by a scenic designer friend who painted a splendid and unusual mural along one wall. It was a splendid jungle scene in the style of Rousseau, with lots of lush green and blue jungle and tigers peering out between huge sea flowers. It certainly cheered the cabin up and gave it a glamorous air of louche bohemianism. As I was constantly being turfed out of this excellent cabin by admirals and their staff, I often wondered what they thought about this work of art. It wasn't obscene and they seemed to suffer it, but strangely enough it was never mentioned.

So, with Fighter Direction I had found myself a nice little private navy, with my comfortable cabin, my mural, friends, bridge, concert parties and the occasional bout of fishing when we were in port and every now and then fighting the war. During a short visit to England for a refit, an attempt was made to haul me away from all this—as by this time I had had active experience—and make me an instructor. I didn't care for that idea at all and put in a plea to remain with *Illustrious*. The Admiralty took pity on me and all I had to do in the way of training meanwhile was give one lecture to impress the young trainees at Yeovilton.

At some stage in 1943 we called in at Durban for a refit. I thoroughly enjoyed myself. When we were in port I had gone ashore and made myself known to the South African Broadcasting Company, who happily gave me some work. One of the nice girls who produced programmes for the company was Yolande D'hotman. We had a great thing . . . She danced beautifully and I was a good dancer in those days. We had a wonderful time and I was very disappointed to leave her.

The South Africans were most hospitable and organized a rota of activities for us, offering sailing, fishing, big-game hunting and anything in which we might be interested. I opted for the trout fishing and went to stay with some extremely kind people called Fergusson who lived up in the Drakensberg. After a bunk, it was heaven to sleep in a real bed and to use silver teapots again, go fishing, and enjoy good company and sunshine. I remember South Africa with great affection and always thought I should love to go back but one realises what an unhappy country it has become, or perhaps always has been. It didn't appear unhappy to us, of course; we were sailors ashore having a wonderful time and we sailed regretfully away, waving damp handkerchiefs.

Off we went to Mombasa. We had been thrown out of Ceylon by the Chinese and we buggered about the Indian Ocean carrying out operations against the Andaman Islands, Java and Sumatra. Then the fleet assembled off the northeast coast of Australia. By this time I was the senior Flight Direction Officer. Either somebody must have thought a good deal of me or I must have given off a lot of confidence, though I reckon I was probably acting my way through it. I also had the right voice, which was not particularly commanding but had the right timbre over the air. The only time I lost any pilots was in the Mediterranean, when something went wrong with the communications. I lost touch with them but if you are flying in the Med and you get lost, you either go north and land in Europe or south and land safely in Africa which they did.

It was about this time that, not only had I formed a deep and lasting attachment to *Illustrious*, but I had also formed a deep and lasting attachment to Eve Mortimer, the young actress I had met four years before at Bristol rep. The ship was in Liverpool having a refit, Eve was working at Southport rep nearby, which had opened again, and, as I had a fortnight's leave, it seemed the perfect opportunity to get married. So, on 27 April 1943, with dear Canon Hudson officiating and Cyril Luckham my best man, Eve and I were married. Eve's mother was not able to come to the wedding. She was a Christian Scientist and, refusing treatment for an illness, was confined to her room. We called to see her after the wedding, had a glass of wine together and then joined *Illustrious*, where a splendid reception had been prepared in the wardroom. The ship's officers and the captain drank our health. We had planned to spend our wedding night in the Adelphi in Liverpool but, as there was some delay with the car that had been sent to fetch us, the captain kindly offered his magnificent cabin for our first dinner together as man and wife, diplomatically getting himself invited down to the wardroom for his dinner. Eve and I were left alone looking at each other across the captain's table in this magnificent cabin, which had been redecorated and furnished by Admiral Mountbatten when he had been in command of the ship.

We spent some of our honeymoon (on a fishing holiday, of course) at Mein Turog in Wales. I don't remember a great deal of the fishing!

I have had a lot of affairs during my life. I have enjoyed the female body but I really don't know what it is to be passionately in love. I loved Eve as much as, if not more than, I have ever loved anyone. Even so, I remember sitting on the train from Liverpool to Mein Turog the morning after we were married, looking across the carriage at Eve and wondering if I had done the right thing. Here we were, married for life. I found the whole idea rather daunting and wondered how common this feeling was. I still do.

After our honeymoon, I went back to *Illustrious* and shortly after sailed away, leaving my bride with a moist handkerchief and a brave smile, ready to go back to her work at Southport rep.

When Germany was defeated in 1945, Fighter Direction, the little private navy of which I was one of the first twelve members, had expanded to several hundred, and after serving on *Illustrious* for two and a half years, I found myself in the Admiralty. I was in the department of the Naval Assistant to the Second Sea Lord and in the powerful position of being able to appoint other Fighter Direction Officers. 'Bigger fleas have little fleas upon their back to bite 'em. Little fleas have smaller fleas and so ad infinitum . . .'

Eve and I had taken a rather grand flat in Elvaston Place in Kensington, and I was enjoying my new desk job. I smoked a lot, telephoned a lot and drank a good deal of gin. I wasn't particularly brilliant at the actual 'deskery' of it, but I suppose I wasn't too bad and it kept me in touch with 'all the bleeding officers, all the bleeding time'. I had quite a jolly time keeping myself busy with three hundred officers to look after and push around the world. A lot of creeping and crawling went on, people coming in and hoping I would appoint them to somewhere nice, handy and comfortable. Quite a few actors were employed in the Fighter Direction Office as we were expected to be good at radio telephoning, speaking into microphones and that sort of thing. One of the officers for whom I was responsible was fellow actor Kenny Moore, who had passed out of Yeovilton with flying colours as a Fighter Direction Officer. His career in films looked very promising and, as the war in Europe had ended and he didn't want to be stuck out in the Pacific, he pleaded with me to find him a job at home. So good was he at his job that I had no choice but to send him out to the Far East. He was rather cross about that but soon came back and all was well; he made a very successful career, generously forgiving me and bearing no malice. We have laughed about it since.

After four years of being kindly looked after by the Navy I realized I was going to have to make my own living. I was four and a half years older than when I had started out. Getting back to my profession became the object and preoccupation of the day. Civvy Street loomed. I have been fortunate with good luck all my life. There I was, being adequately paid by the Navy, with a good deal of time on my hands that I could fill with preparation for my professional life, which was about to start again. Trotting regularly off to the BBC in my naval uniform, I did a good deal of 'moonlight' broadcasting. So, when the curtain finally fell on the Japanese war and I was demobilised, I was in a fairly good position to carry on with my career.

Gordon Harbord was my agent. He was a very well-known name, though not a very high-powered agent, and he looked after a great many struggling actors, myself included. For the first two years after I was demobbed, almost all my income came from radio broadcasting. Consequently I met a good many directors and made many good contacts. There were some great people working for the BBC: Dylan Thomas, John Betjeman, Louis MacNeice. Many actors were still to be demobbed and, as I was a fairly healthy-sounding chap, it was a great time for me. Television had not yet grabbed the public and radio was very popular.

Eve and I moved out of our flat in Elvaston Place and into a very small flat in West Hampstead, more suited to the modest income of a struggling actor. My old chum Malcolm Baker Smith, who had been such a leading light in the entertainments on *Illustrious*, was now doing very well for himself in this exciting new medium, television. He was brave enough to give me the part of Noah in the play of that name by Andre Obey, which was a very big production at Alexandra Palace. This was my first television part and almost my last; it nearly killed me. I knew nothing about television or how it worked.

As a way of familiarizing technicians and staff with this exciting new technique, the 'play of the week' was done twice with two different teams of technicians. The first performance was presented on Sunday night and the whole thing was then repeated again later in the week. It was all live in those days. Using two studios to perform the play, doors were held open as actors dashed along corridors from a scene in one studio to the next studio, holding on grimly to skirts, beards, costume and character, and praying that they wouldn't miss the next scene. It was exhausting. I remember Malcolm taking me home to our little flat in West Hampstead and my collapsing on the floor, whether from exhaustion or the demon drink I am not sure (I have always drunk too much) but it was a great experience. For all this I was paid £45.

Our daughter Joanna was born at Queen Charlotte's Hospital in November 1946 and her first home was our cold little flat in West Hampstead. Food and other rationing were at their worst and strictest in the year after the war ended and 1946 was a desperately cold winter. With almost no fuel and no food, it was not the best time to bring a baby into the world. Eve, who was not very strong, had had a very bad time having Joanna so we employed a monthly nurse to help out, a very powerful lady whom Eve unfortunately didn't get on with at all. However, I think the nurse probably saved Joanna's life, for she was a delicate baby and this powerful woman used to take her into her own bed each night to keep her warm in that bitterly cold winter.

Deciding the tiny flat was no longer suitable for us, we looked around for something larger. We had no money but we had a marvellous bank manager who was very gallant with his lady customers and had a very soft spot for Eve. Those were the days when bank managers were friends and he used to come round at Christmas time with bottles of wine for his favourite clients. He must have had accounts worth millions, but he would come and visit us in our horrid flat. Although I had 'nothing to declare but my talent', he just hoped he was backing a winner and he lent us the money to buy our first house, 49 North Road, Highgate.

I don't know what we paid for that first house. It must have been something pretty enormous like £3000. It was a lovely little Georgian cottage, one of a pair of workmen's cottages between a pub and a garage right on the top of Highgate. It must have been the highest little house in London and we boasted proudly that the highest land to the east were the Ural Mountains. Being the highest house it was also one of the coldest, but we were terribly excited and we loved it with its tiny little garden at the back and little fenced bit at the front, just big enough in which to put Joanna's pram. Those were happy days.

CHAPTER 5

A World Elsewhere

My first stage play after the war was the part of Torvald Helmer in *A Doll's House* at the Intimate Theatre, Palmers Green, Directed by Ronnie Kerr. Having not used my voice, or my body for that matter, in the theatre for over five years, I was anxious about the condition of my vocal chords and sought out the help of a very well-known voice coach who lived near Wigmore Street. This was the only professional training I have ever had and, after seven or eight lessons, I left her. There were quite a few teachers at that time who had a very strong influence on some actors who felt unable to move without first consulting them. Harry Andrews, an actor particularly influenced in this way, wouldn't take a step in his career without first consulting his guru. I didn't fancy that dependence at all so I didn't complete the course but I think that, by teaching me to breathe properly, the lady saved my career. Stage fright used to tighten me up terribly and I would surely have ended up with that scourge of all actors who misuse their voice, the dreaded nodule.

From Torvald in *A Doll's House* I went on to the Aldwych Theatre to be murdered by Terence De Marney in the first act of a play called *Dear Murderer*. He murdered me by leading a tube from a gas fire into a black bag that was placed over my head. Terence De Marney was a real name in those days, a real old ham and a lovely man, but I don't think he would last five minutes in the theatre today. I was very proud to be his understudy and even played his part for two weeks.

Playing opposite me as the detective was Jack Rayne, about whom I remember two things, apart from the fact that he obviously disliked me. He was constantly pointing out defects in my theatrical technique. 'Michael,' he would say, 'I hope you don't mind but in the theatre, if we pass another actor on stage, we usually cross from behind.' There was also another strange maxim about never being supposed to move when another actor was speaking. Jack was also one of the first people who have ever suggested that I might be a touch on the mean side. I was always running out of cigarettes and this happened one night at the Theatre Royal, Bath. I called in at his dressing room to scrounge a fag. Holding out the packet he said, 'There you are, you mean bugger.' I was terribly shocked and said, 'Do you mean that?' to which he replied, 'Well, since you ask, yes I do.' After that I took great care always to have a supply of cigarettes.

A year or two later, I was the only Englishman in a play on Broadway called *Moonbirds*. I was playing the lead so I was an important sort of chap and I remember going into a Broadway production office and seeing a lot of small-part actors waiting to be interviewed in the vestibule. One of them was Jack Rayne. He didn't get a part but I don't suppose he minded much as the play only ran on Broadway for two nights. It had been beset with terrible problems and clashes of personality and finally, when we got to Broadway, and I saw my name in lights I thought, '*well, I have arrived*'. I went to the first-night party and read the notices and almost immediately the play closed. I didn't 'arrive' for long; they didn't even put my name up the second night because they wanted to save on the electricity bill.

1946 was also the year of *Passport to Pimlico*, a charming and hugely popular film which greatly appealed to the British sense of patriotism and identity. It was a film which exactly captured the post-war feeling and people loved it. London at that time had not been rebuilt at all and we made the film in the middle of bomb-damaged Pimlico. I played a splendid policeman, very tense and hyperactive, as I suspect most of my performances in those days were too. I met and fell in love with Barbara Murray, who was at the beginning of her career. She was a Rank starlet, a beautiful girl, lovely and real, whom I was to work with again years later at the Aldwych Theatre in *The Collection* by Harold Pinter.

Later that year, my old friend Malcolm Baker Smith turned up trumps again and had me playing Bottom at Covent Garden in Constant Lambert's new 1946 production of Purcell's *Fairy Queen*. It was a vast and complicated affair with Robert Helpmann playing Oberon and Margaret Rawlings, Titania; the choreographer was Frederick Ashton and the set and costume designer Michael Ayrton. Helpmann wore an extra-ordinary headdress fashioned like a chrysalis from which he emerged to strut around the stage in obligatory ballet tights, casting baleful glances at Margaret Rawlings—concluding (rightly) that she was too heavy to lift and consequently making no attempt to dance at all. In addition, we had a vast chorus of singers and dancers, including Beryl Grey and Gillian Lynne, who later became an international choreographer. And I see from the original cast list that 'A Nymph' was danced by one Moira Shearer and amongst the Spirits of the Air were

Margot Fonteyn and Michael Somes. They performed all manner of bird ballets, night masques and seasonal frolics which altogether left the three of us (myself, Helpmann and Rawlings) as the primary speaking parts rather upstaged. I certainly felt much happier when I could hide behind my vast ass's head—I think my performance rather went downhill when I had to take it off. Constant Lambert wrote me a little song, so there I was on the stage at Covent Garden, singing a solo;

The Ousle cock so black of hue with orange tawny bill,
The Throstle with his note so true, the wren with little
  quill . . .

Constant Lambert kindly wrote at the bottom of the music, 'To be sung in any key'.

Noose was written by Richard Llewellyn, the author of *How Green Was My Valley*. It was a very topical story about actors coming home from the war and trying to get their lives together. I played the gallant Captain Hoyle, Nigel Patrick the Adjutant, and we both played opposite a beautiful girl, Patricia Hilliard, with whom I used to flirt madly in the bar after the show. Pat was rather flat-chested and I didn't have much of a figure so we stuffed the tops of our clothes with newspaper in order to make ourselves more substantial. When we came into a crunch, it really was a crunch. This was presented at the Saville Theatre, which is now a cinema, directed by Reginald Tate. I acquired some very strange notices for my performance, the *Sunday Times* saying, 'Mr Hordern plays the gallant hero with his tongue anywhere but in his cheek'.

By now my agent was Al Parker whose partner, Montie Mackie, largely looked after me. She and Al had a junior called Ronnie Waters who gradually became my particular chap and in fact has been my agent ever since, and a very good agent too.

By now the work was fairly starting to roll in. In 1948, amongst film and radio work, I did a play by Peter Ustinov called *The Indifferent Shepherd* at the Q Theatre, a little theatre opposite Kew Bridge station. This was followed by Pastor Manders in Ibsen's *Ghosts* directed by Willard Stoker. The year ended with Mr Toad in *The Wind in the Willows* at the Shakespeare Memorial Theatre, Stratford.

This was a very energetic show which opened in the Christmas of 1948, directed by John Kidd, with an enormous cast of local children playing stoats, ferrets, rabbits, fieldmice, etc. The main characters were played by members of the Shakespeare company left over from the season. Michael Gwynn played Badger marvellously, that volatile actor William Squire, Ratty, and a little man called Bertram Shuttleworth played Mole. He later gave up the business to run a bookshop, a very appropriate occupation for a mole I thought. Andrew Faulds was Chief Weasel, Michael Bates, Chief Ferret, and I, in a green Dutch cap and rubber cheeks, played Mr Toad.

I adored that show. It was wonderful and exhausting—so much so that the local doctor used to call in at the theatre twice a week to give me a reviving shot of vitamins to keep me leaping about. This little extract from Grahame's classic book brings it all back to me:

The motor car went Poop-poop-poop
   As it raced along the road.
Who was it steered it into a pond?
   Ingenious Mr Toad

'O, how clever I am! How clever, how very cle —'
   A slight noise at a distance behind him made him turn his head and look. O horror! O misery! O despair!
   About two fields off a chauffeur in his leather gaiters and two large rural policemen were visible, running towards him as hard as they could go!

Poor Toad sprang to his feet and pelted away again, his heart in his mouth. 'O my!' he gasped, as he panted along, 'what an ass I am! What a conceited and heedless ass! Swaggering again; Shouting and singing songs again! Sitting still and gassing again! O my! O my! O my!'

We had very good notices and it was an extraordinarily rewarding show, a good deal of it being quite spontaneous. It was exciting going into the theatre every evening; one was on a great high seeing people pouring in and knowing they were going to have a good time. Eve was also in the production playing the nurse and the washerwoman. I know she enjoyed it as much as I did and we loved working together again. On the first night, the little weasels, stoats and assorted animals gave me as a first-night present, a little Victorian brass stud box in the shape of a toad and I told them that I would always keep it on my dressing room table wherever I was working to remind me that, however tired I was when I was playing Lear or Prospero, I was never as tired and as hard-worked as when I was playing Mr Toad at Stratford. It still shares my dressing room today.

We repeated this performance the following year with very few cast changes, though Alan Badel took over from Bill Squire to play a rather sinister version of Ratty. Then it was decided to take the production to the Princess Theatre, London. By this time, realizing what hard work it was, I stuck my fee up quite considerably, Leo McKern was offered the part and I cheerfully stood down.

My fishing diary for 23 April 1948 reads:

Caught the 5.55 at Paddington after the television matinee of *Libel*. Coming straight from Alexandra Palace I met Eve on the train, got seats and restaurant car tickets then retired to the gents' wash and brush up with my bottle of shampoo and took off my grey hair—coming in grey and going out normal the chap in charge was very intrigued. Hired a car from Abergavenny and reached the usual welcome at Glawcoed at about 11 pm. A glorious warm starlit night and the smell of the spring after London beyond description.

Spring 1949 brought *A Woman in Love*, translated from the French and directed by Michael Redgrave. I remember it chiefly because I had the best part, playing the family friend, Pascal. Redgrave played Germaine, a famous author, opposite Margaret Rawlings. Unfortunately they really did not get on well at all and the relationship disintegrated to reach such a low ebb that they were soon refusing to speak to each other. Communication was by means of notes of the 'would you mind not killing my laugh' variety, which made things all very difficult. Michael had hoped it would go to the West End and help revive his at that time flagging financial state, but no, it was not to be.

Later in the year, this was followed by a poetic drama called *Stratton* by Ronnie Duncan, with music by Benjamin Britten. Poetic drama was all the rage in 1949, Christopher Fry being very fashionable. Again I had the best part, playing the Reverend John Courtenay opposite a well-known film actor, Clive Brook, who was not a humble chap and used to complain loudly when characters in a play were not entirely concentrating on him.

April 1950 brought a turning point in my career. I was asked to play Nikolai Ivanov in a production of *Ivanov* at the Arts Theatre, Cambridge, directed by John Fernald. It hadn't been produced in this country for twenty-five years so there was something of an air of theatrical expectancy about it.

Ivanov is a self-pitying character who is incapable of happiness and it is difficult for an audience to feel entirely sympathetic towards this self-destructive hero but T. C. Worsley felt I had made quite a good job of it. He wrote:

> Perhaps an actor with star quality might have imposed on us more sucessfully than Mr Michael Hordern, and won our sympathy for Ivanov by his own personality. But such a performance would have raised the level of expectation all round. As it is, Mr Hordern is rich in intelligence, sensitivity and grasp, and with very few exceptions, the company give his impressive playing the right kind of support.

This was immediately followed by *Macbeth*, directed by Alec Clunes who also played the leading role and I gave my Macduff. Lady Macbeth was played by Margaret Rawlings with 'ebony and ivory beauty' and the ghost rising out of Macbeth's chair was played with 'innate nobility of spirit' by Eric Berry. My Macduff was, according to the critic Audrey Williamson, 'deeply moving, his

> If thou beest slain and with no stroke of mine
> My wife and children's ghosts will haunt me still

sounding a note of truly haunted grief'.

But on the whole this production was not well received by the critics. Is *Macbeth* ever? In October that year I went on to the Prince's Theatre to play Christopher in *Party Manners* and in September 1951, I was back at the Arts Theatre playing Paul Southman in *Saint's Day*.

A play by a new young writer John Whiting, *Saint's Day* was one of three winners in a competition at the Arts Theatre, London, organized by Alec Clunes. I don't recall who the other playwrights were but the prizes for the three winners were to have their plays produced by a professional company at the Arts Theatre.

John Whiting was a lovely man. Being terribly shy, he found it quite difficult to talk to people, so he and I got on splendidly. If you asked him why he had written such and such a line, he was absolutely floored and quite unable to explain. He had already had produced a delicate, imaginative play called *A Penny for a Song*, (though *Saint's Day* was written before it), which had been directed by Peter Brook but which for some inexplicable reason had failed at the Haymarket Theatre. But it gave a strong indication of his powers as a playwright and his new play was awaited with some interest.

Saint's Day was a bitter, interesting play. It was produced by Stephen Murray and I played the lead, a marvellous part of a chap as old as Methuselah. The script was way ahead of its time. When I was offered the part I took a deep breath and thought, 'I don't know what this play is all about, but this is obviously a part I mustn't refuse.' It's a very difficult and obscure play, but I think there is a level on which one can act a part without necessarily needing to understand the play at all. To a large extent it's quite a good thing that the actor shouldn't know what the author's basic intention is. If the author is committed in some way and is putting this over, then I think it's a mistake to be too involved.

It attracted a good deal of notice as it was Whiting's first play and a great many well-known people came to see it. It was greeted with derision by the critics, who said it was turgid and pretentious. What was the Arts Theatre thinking of? Was this the future of English drama? And so on and so on. In the teeth of this criticism, the Arts Theatre bravely awarded *Saint's Day* first prize. It was, I believe, an honest gesture to award one of the most sought-after theatrical prizes to a play which had been so hugely slated. The notices it got were disgraceful and provoked many people, amongst them John Gielgud and Laurence Olivier, to write angry letters to the press saying that the notices were quite wrong and that this play was a milestone in the theatre and everyone should come and see it. I came across some thoughts of the eminent critic J. C. Trewin about the play, penned after he had watched it at a matinée in a half-empty theatre.

I came into the clanging street, baffled yet haunted, oppressed, unable to throw off the weight of that dark house, that tortured world of query and symbol, and I wondered whether it could be right to dismiss simply as turgid nonsense a play that had so powerful an effect upon the mind; one that clung and would not release its hold. The question remained unresolved. There it was: the First Prizewinner, the enigma of *Saint's Day*: crowned by three distinguished men of the theatre, applauded by two others in letters to *The Times*, damned by the critics: a play libelled and rejected. In my heart I could not reject it. When I recall some of the successful plays of our time, I am glad I have known *Saint's Day*, to set it above these polite tepid timidities. It still flares smokily in the recollection. It makes me believe that John Whiting may be one day a dramatist of the first rank. He has far to go but, himself a Grand Old Man, he may yet strip his sleeve and show his scars and say, 'Those were the wounds of *Saint's Day*— long ago'. Do not, I beg of you, forget his name.

This all created a lot of publicity, doing me a power of good at the same time, encouraging Glen Byam Shaw to offer me an incredible clutch of plays at Stratford the following season at what was then the Shakespeare Memorial Theatre. I was offered the parts of Caliban in *The Tempest*, Jacques in *As You Like It* and Sir Politick Would-Be in Ben Jonson's *Volpone*. I suppose it was a good turning point for me. I always think of a career as an arm with wrist, elbow and shoulder; this was a change of direction, a change of angle, an elbow.

I was fairly shaken by Glen's offer. I didn't know much about

91

Shakespeare and I remember ringing up Violet Lamb, Cyril Luckham's wife, an old friend from Bristol days, who knew about plays and 'the drama' and she was very shaken also. 'I've been offered a part called Caliban in *The Tempest* and I can't make out what sort of chap he is,' I quavered. Her reaction was 'Caliban?, Jacques? And you're hesitating?'

Anthony Quayle was gradually handing over the reins of the Shakespeare Memorial Theatre, Stratford, to Byam Shaw, a splendid director who had started his career as an actor. He had been appointed director of the Old Vic School and Theatre Centre and his work had largely been in developing that organization. He had a very good reputation as a director, working with people like Edith Evans, John Gielgud and Godfrey Tearle, and was now making a name for himself at Stratford. He, together with Quayle, bravely offered me these splendid parts for the following Stratford season. I did know something of *As You Like It*, as years before I had played Orlando as an amateur and so I knew roughly what 'Jacques' was about but as for Caliban, Menenius in *Coriolanus* and Volpone's Sir Politick Would-Be, I had no idea and had to say to Glen, 'I think I had better confess now that these parts mean nothing to me.' Glen's reaction was, 'That's splendid, wonderful, promise me you won't read up anything about them. Read the plays as much as you like but don't read commentators and critics.' Being a lazy bugger, I was only too pleased to say 'Yes certainly'. I had no wish to sit up burning the midnight oil and that is how I approached every part I ever played, King Lear included.

Eve, Joanna and I found accommodation in Goldicote House, a large country house three miles on the London side of Stratford. Joanna went to a local Stratford school and we lived a very happy country existence. I used to go pigeon shooting in the Goldicote woods. Some of the cast, including Siobhan McKenna and Laurence Harvey, used to come out and babysit. It was a happy season.

Glen Byam Shaw was a marvellous director. But I was aware that I was following the Menenius of Alec Guinness, which had caused quite a stir four years before in a 1948 revival of *Coriolanus* with the Old Vic Company at the New Theatre. I remember during rehearsals for *Coriolanus* I wasn't getting on very well as Menenius. I just couldn't get the aristocracy of the man, the self-confidence, the patriotism. On the day of the dress rehearsals, when my confidence was at an all-time low and I was near despair, Glen took me out to the theatre restaurant for lunch, bought an extremely expensive bottle of claret, we ate a splendid meal and it just did the trick. It was the bit of production that I needed, good wine was just the sort of thing Menenius would know all about.

I was flattered to receive these words of encouragement from Michael Redgrave.

My dear Michael,

We had to rush away after 'Volpone' and I have been regretting ever since that it should have been only after 'As You Like It' that I came round to see you, when I ventured to make a slight criticism. Your Caliban is immensely fine, with all the pity and pathos, which last year were so heavily over-loaded that they became soggy, but with real terror and humour as well. Sir Politick is, as I believe has been said, nothing short of a revelation. I wish you were going to be with us next year, but whatever you do, I shall always wish you well.

Much love to Eve and to you
Michael.

One critic was kind enough to suggest that my Menenius Agrippa looks in profile strangely like early portraits of Frank Benson, Stratford's patron saint. Mr Hordern's Menenius is a dryly acute study of the 'humorous patrician' and one moreover that can move our compassion in the Volscian cameo. We had felt that it would be long before Alec Guinness's Menenius could be matched. The fact that Michael Hordern's different reading can now stand beside the other does credit to a player who will be a Stratford prize.

The 1952 company was exciting, a strong bunch of actors, Ralph Richardson, Margaret Leighton, Laurence Harvey, Mary Ellis, Siobhan McKenna, George Devine directing *Volpone*, John Gielgud directing Richardson in *Macbeth*, Michael Benthall directing *The Tempest* and Glen directing *Coriolanus* and *As You Like It*. Motley, Loudon Sainthill and Michael Northern were amongst the designers and much of the incidental music was composed by Antony Hopkins.

Ralph Richardson was a dear old boy but he terrified me. He could be very savage and I had learnt a few lessons from leading actors: '. . . normally on stage, Hordern, we cross behind other actors . . .'. He was terribly good as Volpone, but not so successful at Macbeth.

This was my play out and I had been away fishing in Wales. Coming back to see the first night, I called in at the theatre to watch some of the dress rehearsal. I could not believe what I was seeing. It was an awful mishmash, with Gielgud trying to direct and Richardson saying, 'I don't understand old boy'. Poor Ralph was in an awful state. In the fight at the end with Macduff, going 'one, two, three, oh my dear chap, four, five six', he was terrible. I went home to Eve that night and said, 'They will have to have a diplomatic illness. They cannot take money and show this to the public tomorrow.' But they did the next night, and it got the most appalling notices. Ralph was 'adrift', as we used to say in the Navy. The next day, going into the theatre to collect his mail, Ralph met fellow actor Raymond Westwall, who, being immersed in his own mail and not noticing Ralph, completely ignored him. That evening in the theatre, before going on stage, Ralph turned to the unfortunate Raymond and said, 'You cut me this morning. If you do that again I will put it about in London that you played Banquo to my Macbeth.' He had a wonderful sense of humour, but I was very frightened of him. He could be distressingly autocratic and dismissive. I played Caliban opposite his Prospero and he was lost there too. I think one of the reasons for Ralph's failure was that he was a bit off-beam during that season. He always had an endearing, attractive vagueness, but he was a bit scattier than usual that year because he had been distracted, and small blame to him, by Margaret Leighton who, playing Ariel to his Prospero pranced around him with very few clothes on, looking utterly enchanting. He was determined to have a love affair with her but her heart belonged to Laurence Harvey and, when the time came to play opposite her in *Macbeth*, it all proved too much of a strain.

It was a very pleasant summer. I had got to know the river a bit during the *Toad* season four years before and used to fish in a tributary of the Avon which came down from Goldicote. It had no trout but plenty of roach, perch and dace so, when not rehearsing, there I would be digging for worms, fishing, throwing everything back except the perch, which were delicious. It was a nice town and country life, the excitement and sophistication of the theatre in the evening the perfect counterpart to digging for worms and fishing during the day.

When the season ended in October, we regretfully packed everything up and it was 'up anchor' and back to our little house in Highgate. I was almost immediately headhunted by

Michael Benthall to go and play more Shakespeare in the 1953–54 season at the Old Vic. He had just taken over as artistic director and I felt as though my star was rising. If I didn't know anything about Shakespeare before, I was certainly getting the chance to catch up now. The Old Vic had a five-year plan to produce all thirty-six plays in the First Folio. On 14 September 1953 we opened with *Hamlet* which we took to the Edinburgh Festival before transferring to London. In shape and design the Assembly Hall in Edinburgh was vastly different from the Old Vic theatre. A long rectangular stage jutted out into the audience, who sat on three sides. There was much dashing about throughout the play; as we had such a vast stage to get across, some of our exits and entrances seemed to go on for ever. We must have looked frightfully funny trying desperately to come in on cue as we breathlessly crossed the stage while attempting to make it all seem effortless and natural. Alan Dent called it 'Hamlet at the White City', which aptly highlighted the problem. Back in London, we returned to a more conventional stage; the critics proved much kinder and seemed to find something in the production which had been obscured at the Festival. The production had been revised and we had all gained from the Edinburgh experience. By the time it got to The Old Vic the production had settled down and was really rather good. Apart from myself as Polonius, it was a glittering cast, Richard Burton giving his Hamlet; Claire Bloom as Ophelia, Fay Compton as Gertrude, my old friend Bill Squire as Horatio; John Neville as Fortinbras; another old friend Pat Ide doing publicity and Clifford Williams, who years later at Stratford was to direct me in *The Tempest*, was Player Queen. Burton was a notable Hamlet and Fay Compton outstanding as Gertrude. About me the critics were not quite so sure:

'Michael Hordern chose Hamlet's description of a "foolish prating knave" as a clue to Polonius; fussy and meddlesome, but endearing, he was at his best in his early scenes with

Ophelia before he began to obscure less matter with more art.'

On tour with The Old Vic company in 1954, when we were playing in Newcastle and staying at the Angler's Arms, Weldon Bridge, Morpeth, I see from my fishing diary that my obsession with fishing was getting in the way of any thespian concentration. The Coquet is a beautiful clean river and the country delightful. The Northumberland Anglers' Federation has miles of water conveniently fished by car from the Angler's Arms. It was strange to be doffing waders on the riverbank in the evening and making up for Malvolio or Polonius less than an hour later. In fact one night my mind was so on the river that I started making up for Malvolio only to be told at the ¼ that it was a Hamlet night . . .

Hamlet was the perfect play with which to open the season as it has such fine strong parts for everyone and is a good showpiece for an actor's latent vanity. It had a very successful run and enjoyed a hundred and one performances. This placed Richard as *Hamlet* in the ranks of such greats as Sir Henry Irving, Sir John Gielgud and Sir Herbert Beerbohm Tree, the only other actors to have played the part a hundred times in any one run. The sets were almost blindingly colourful and adventurous in design. In the centre of the stage was a flight of stairs leading off into black oblivion which seemed to swallow up the actor as he exited. It gave the impression of an entrance into the raging battlements which sparked the play with a wonderfully threatening feeling of impending war. We knew it was a good production, finer than our opening days in Edinburgh, strongly directed with Michael Benthall at the helm.

So it was with some enthusiasm that we took *Hamlet* later that year to Elsinore and performed before three crowned heads of Scandinavia. Ironically, it was Claire Bloom and not Richard who captivated the Scandinavian audience, though there were fine performances from all. During the reception, I found myself talking to King Augustus of Sweden, who said that he often came over to Elsinore as it was only twenty minutes on the ferry. Knowing him to be a keen fisherman, I soon got him onto the subject of fish. We spent the entire reception boring each other to death with fishing stories!

Richard Burton was not an heroic figure of a man. He was stocky and short, with terrible legs in tights. In this 1953–54 season he had been cast against type, which was a very good experience for him but meant that he was not always very good at some of the parts he had to play and gave some lazy performances. While in Edinburgh, *Punch* somewhat maliciously, I thought, quoted T. S. Eliot's Prufrock: 'No! I am not Prince Hamlet, nor was meant to be'.

These proved merely to be teething problems for Richard and once in London his performance matured. It was a gruelling season but he was adamant that he should play the part. After seeing the production a second time, this time in London, *The Times* theatre critic remarked:

> Mr Burton's playing of Hamlet in the new surroundings has become something altogether different . . . at every fascinating turn of a performance which is satisfying as any that memory can recall for a great many years.

Richard was an immensely likeable man, with marvellous charm and charisma so that he could get away with anything. The audience adored him and night after night there would be a crowd outside the stage door, filling the street right to the other side of the road. Out I would come, having given my King John, Parolles or Prospero and having collected some splendid notices, to be quite unrecognised, whilst Burton would be besieged by admirers. We had a sort of love-hate relationship because I felt that he was a bit incensed that I had collected good notices whilst obviously not exciting the audience as he did. There were many occasions when we'd be in the pub together and he'd suddenly get quite ratty with me. There was undoubtedly friction between us. I was also jealous of him and acutely envious of his wonderful power over the audience. I realized that a commodity Burton had that I hadn't was sex appeal. He simply oozed sexuality and women just went wild. Afterwards, when he became a big Hollywood star and was playing tremendous parts, I was moved by his kindness in remembering his friends from the Old Vic days and making sure we joined him in some of his films.

I made about six films with him, amongst them *Alexander the Great*, *Cleopatra* and *The Spy Who Came in from the Cold*. He had a tremendous literary mind and a store of literature in his head, but it would not have mattered if he had or not; all he had to do was walk on stage, open his mouth and speak and the audience was his. There was no stage trickery in Burton's performance besides the lilting Welsh melancholy which was hugely effective. There was a specially wonderful moment on the stage when he spoke the 'too solid flesh' soliloquy with such blinding sadness and humility that one could not fail to be moved.

The big shock of the season for me was *King John*. The title role was to be played by an actor who proved totally inexperienced, and after a week or two of rehearsals it became obvious that he was not going to manage it. I was approached to play the part. This was a bit of a shaker as it is a difficult part in a difficult play and I already had quite a lot on my plate with the three Ps, Prospero, Parolles and Polonius. However, my actor's vanity would not let me turn down such a marvellous chance and, with optimism unusual for me, I said I would have a go, forgetting I was already caught up with a film at Pinewood, something I would never have tackled had I known I was going to play King John! However, the contract was signed, so I had to go ahead with it all. I have discovered over the years that this situation is quite typical of an actor's life, one is either sitting around doing nothing, waiting for the phone to ring (or in my case fishing all day), or working oneself into the ground. Anyway, there it was, I was committed to all this work and I went to it with a will.

King John stands alone among the histories as a purely medieval play that does not touch the world of the other historical plays. It is a difficult play in the sense that it has no common purpose or apparent theme. But, thanks to George Devine, the producer who had a very clear vision of the play, it proved a successful run. 'OLD VIC MAKE BAD KING GOOD PLAY' was the *Glasgow Herald*'s headline and I took this as a great compliment.

All went well until the last night of *King John*, which nearly defeated me. As I was filming every day during the last week of *King John*, my doctor had given me some pep pills, which were very popular in those days, with some instruction to take one six hours before I needed extra energy. It is rather difficult to know how you are going to feel six hours before the curtain goes up and I had resisted taking these pills until the last day. By the end of the week I was on my knees with exhaustion and, six hours before my last performance of *King John*, I decided to take some of these pills. Driving back from Pinewood to the Old Vic that afternoon, I arrived with very little time to spare. Slapping on my not uncomplicated make-up, and with enormous confidence and bravura, I asked my dresser to pop out and bring back a bottle of champagne. Feeling tremendously confident, I downed a glass or two with huge enjoyment and strode out on stage to play what I considered to be the definitive performance of King John. In my dressing room after the show, enjoying the rest of the champagne and feeling very pleased with myself, I prepared for the paeans of praise from Eve, who had been watching the last night. Her face, as she stood in the doorway of my dressing room, was, as they say, a picture. She was aghast, horrified. 'What were you doing?' she said, 'You were simply terrible, all over the place. What on earth was wrong with you?'

After that I was very careful never again to mix acting with alcohol or pills. I must have been speaking garbled rubbish. As King John says as he leans towards Hubert, 'I had a thing to say—but let it go.'

It was a very good lesson.

I was by no means a perfect father and husband, being too self-ish and involved in my work, which I loved, and my fishing, which I loved even more. As my theatrical career began to take off, I suppose I became even more neglectful. So, in order to see me at all, the family had to join me by the side of a stream. Joanna, by now six or seven, used to come fishing with me a good deal. I don't really think it was the actual fishing which fascinated her but she used to enjoy just being around me and hearing my exclamations of delight or frustration and simply being in the countryside, walking in a chalk stream or picking flowers. Out of this grew a love of the countryside which she has today.

Eve loved the countryside too and knew a good deal about wild flowers, teaching Joanna all their names. But Eve was a much more sociable person than I. She loved London and going to the theatre, out to dinner, meeting friends, and doing all the usual civilized things normal people enjoy. But, poor girl, she was sadly hampered by a most unsociable husband who was little interested in entertaining or meeting people, not a sociable chap at all—too mean and too selfish, I suppose. So we did very little of the going about together which she would have enjoyed.

It was Spring 1955 and Rex Harrison was directing a French comedy called *Nina* by André Roussin, a great exponent of boulevard theatre. It was a tale of a husband, a wife and a lover and, although I didn't know it at the time, was a mirror of Rex's own marital breakdown,. which might account for some of the problems we had with it. It had a strong cast with James Hayter and my old friend Lockwood West, and Edith Evans playing the title role. The whole venture was doomed from the beginning and, if I hadn't been so seduced and flattered with the idea of working with such well-known people, I would not have touched it. Everything seemed to go wrong. Edith collapsed during the tour and had to be replaced by an understudy who had omitted to learn her lines and had to go on with the script. The male lead was found to be inadequate for some reason and, answering a frantic phone call from Binkie Beaumont, the impresario, I agreed to take over at a week's notice. At the same time, Rex was attempting to direct the play on tour and perform in *Bell, Book and Candle* in the West End in the evenings. It was all very strange and confusing. After a week's rehearsal with Rex, I joined the company in Oxford; this was a very awkward and embarassing experience as the actor I was about to replace was still playing the part. I should have realized the whole thing had an odd feel about it—but no, ignoring my deepest, gloomiest instincts, I plodded on and a week after I had landed the part, I opened in the play at the Theatre Royal, Brighton.

I don't think I forgot my lines, but it must have been a very strange performance. Edith had decided to recover by this time and rejoin the cast, and we began to rehearse together. It all seemed to be going rather well when, one afternoon when the two of us were working together with a stage manager over-seeing us, Edith, to our great surprise, walked to the side of the stage, looked sadly at the rows of empty seats and announced dramatically, 'I suppose it comes to every actress in time, this is the end of my career'.

The stage manager and I looked on at this performance in amazement, not quite sure what was expected of us. I felt rather hurt, not wanting to believe that she felt like this because my performance was so awful; after all, she had apparently only agreed to come back to the play on condition that I was playing opposite her. I was under the impression that we were getting on rather well and in fact were playing together as though we had known each other for ever. Perhaps she just realized she was much too old for the part. Whatever it was, as we sadly put her into her car, the stage manager and I, I thought to myself, 'Here I am in the centre of a piece of theatrical history, witnessing the demise of one of the greatest actresses in the theatre'.

I needn't have worried. A month or two later, she was back on the boards playing in something much more suitable. It wasn't until I worked with her again years later that I realized how insecure an actress she was. We were rehearsing a well-known scene for a charity gala in front of an audience of cleaners and ushers and I found myself getting some extremely nice laughs out of this select little group. 'This is marvellous,' I thought and felt very pleased with myself. When playing the scene again in the evening in front of the invited audience, Edith managed brilliantly to kill every single laugh that might have been coming my way. So worried was she about being overshadowed that she had perfected the skills of upstaging; cutting in with lines too soon, fidgeting and generally diverting attention from the actor delivering the lines. She was missing the point of the job. I have seen so many actors absolutely pinned down by ambition. They miss an awful lot of fun.

To return to our production of *Nina* in Brighton, the problem now was who was going to take her place. Coral Browne agreed to take over the part and was brought back from a holiday in Majorca, and the whole ghastly process was repeated; a week's rehearsal with Rex and then out on tour to join the rest of the cast.

Until now, I had been the golden boy, saving the day, keeping the flag flying and the curtain up. I could do no wrong, Rex making me feel terribly important and clever, but now all that was changed. I could do nothing right and was constantly being slapped down by Rex; 'If you think you are playing this scene with the understudy, Hordern, you are wrong, this is Miss Brown's scene.'

I felt mortified. *De mortuis nil nisi bonum* and all that – he was impossible. Gone was the charming, sophisticated Rex Harrison and in his place was a bully, a monster. It was agony. All the frustrations and traumas of the production seemed to be heaped upon me. I remember going back to my hotel and, grown man that I was, crying in bed at night, wondering how I could face rehearsal the next morning.

When the company reached Eastbourne, Rex mercifully decided to leave us alone for a few days. Feeling much in need of the warmth and support of my family, I telephoned Eve and Joanna to entice them down with the idea of a seaside holiday. As I met them off the train at Eastbourne, to my horror Rex Harrison stepped out of the next carriage. Avoidance was impossible and, creep that I was, I drove him to his hotel, promising not to divulge his presence to the rest of the cast, who thought he was safely *Bell, Book and Candle*-ing in London!

I acted my socks off that night, but it did me no good. He assembled us afterwards and said cruelly. 'What I have seen tonight is fit only for the end of the pier! I want to see you all tomorrow at ten sharp for rehearsals.' Miserably collecting together the next morning, we were a depressing sight; a more unhappy bunch of thespians it would be hard to imagine. I hadn't slept a wink all night and was feeling more than angry as I believed he was being grossly unfair and that we really

My mother

My father. 'Ned'

Peter, Shrimp and me   *Below* On the wall of the 'quad' at Windlesham

Mummy, Doody, Shrimp and me with the Malden family

Canon Hudson and me
– Shrimp and Peter on either
side at 'The Poplars'

The family off for the summer
holidays

Ned on 'Jimbo' – Doody on the
beastly little pony 'Chloe'

(Back row) Dacia holding
'Mirth', Mummy, me (oranges
in my pocket, I had traded trout
to get them), (Front row) Dacia's
son John, Doody holding
'Treacle Tart', and Peter

Mrs Charles, Shrimp, Peter and me at
Windlesham

Peter, Shrimp and me in the barrow

'Hawk Patrol' of the Boy Scouts – Each patrol had its own railway carriage

Me on the porch at Jordan in about 1922

Barefoot on the 'Francis-Barnett'

Windlesham House first fifteen. I am cross-legged in the centre
– the scrum-half

My first salmon caught at Eagle Rock on
the Double Dart and weighing 10 lb
Inset My machine for smoking fish

Left Eve called this photo 'the shady agent'

Below In this amateur production of R C Sherriffs' *Journey's End* in Stevenage in 1934, I played Raleigh (Centre)

Right Seth in
Cold Comfort Farm
at Bristol, 1938

*Below The Importance
of Being Earnest*, at
Bristol Little Theatre
in 1939, with
Violet Lamb and
Ralph Hutton

A 'Polyfoto' of Acting Able Seaman Hordern on joining the Navy
in 1940

Above Goggling in
Ceylon in 1941

Left Lt/Cdr RNVR Hordern in
Bristol in 1942. I was very
proud of my stripes

Below Our wedding day
April 27, 1943

Left My first appearance
on TV playing Noah
in 1946

Right As Tony Peters in
*What Shall We Tell
Caroline?* (1958) at the
Lyric, Hammersmith
and subsequently at the
Garrick, with
Brenda Bruce

Left Toad of Toad Hall
at Stratford 1949. I am
Toad, with my
daughter Joanna aged 3

Right As Pastor
Manders, with Flora
Robson (Mrs Alving),
in Ibsen's *Ghosts*

Left Macbeth, with
Beatrix Lehmann, at
the Old Vic

Above Polonius, with
Claire Bloom playing
Ophelia, at the Old Vic
1953/54

Above right Sir Politick
Would-Be in *Volpone* at
Stratford in 1952

Right Caliban in
The Tempest at Stratford
in 1952

Margenhall in *The Dock Brief* at the
Garrick, 1958

With Richard Burton in the film of John Le Carré's *The Spy Who Came in from the Cold* (1965). I played the homosexual 'agent provocateur'

King Lear at the Nottingham Playhouse 1969/70 and then at the Old Vic. Penelope Wilton was Cordelia and Peter Eyre played Edgar. Bruce Myles was Albany and Peter Whitbread, Kent

Jumpers, with Julie Covington, at the National Theatre 1976/77

Sir Cedric in *Ivanhoe* (1981) taking a break

Paradise Postponed, John Mortimer's highly successful 1985 television series, with Richard Vernon, Jill Bennett, David Threlfall and Annette Crosbie

Sir Anthony Absolute eating his egg in the 1983/84 National Theatre production of *The Rivals*

With my grandson Nicholas aged 1½ on
Palling beach, Norfolk in February 1985.
Taken by my son-in-law, the photographer,
Fritz Curzon *Inset* Eve

Then, 1919, and now (from left to right) Shrimp, Doody,
me and Peter (who played rugger for England and died in 1987)

On the Lambourn at Bagnor

hadn't done too badly. Rehearsal had hardly begun before he was at it, being sharp and cryptic about me. This was the final straw. I lost my rag. I am not a man given to physical violence but on this occasion I was. I found depths of fury in myself which I had no idea existed in my rather timid frame and it was fortunate for Rex that he was on the other side of the orchestra pit, otherwise I would have hit him. I was screaming a good deal and, the middle of all this confusion, a voice bellowed from in the back of the stalls, 'Michael, Rex, calm down!'

It was the unfortunate Binkie Beaumont who, having sunk a good deal of money into this show, had unexpectedly come down from London to see how his investment was getting on and whether the horror stories he had been hearing were true. They were. Hugh 'Binkie' Beaumont was an enormously successful theatrical impresario. He was managing director of H. M. Tennent Ltd, the production managers, and he was an immensely powerful force in the theatre after the war, making and breaking many careers. He was a shrewd man with an impeccable instinct for matching the right play with the right actor. He was closely associated with John Gielgud during his classical seasons of plays at the Phoenix and the Lyric, in Hammersmith, in the 1950s. Amongst the many successes he put on were *Dear Octopus, The Heiress, Nude with a Violin, Oklahoma, Irma La Douce, West Side Story, Hello, Dolly!* and *My Fair Lady. Nina* was not, however, to be included in this glittering array.

We opened at the Haymarket Theatre, in London, a week later and it was a disaster, closing after five weeks. The play was fine. It was a disaster because of Rex Harrison.

Meeting Coral Browne made up for a good deal of the nightmare of *Nina*. I liked her very much indeed from the first moment I met her. She was terribly attractive, with a marvellous dry sense of humour which got us through many tricky moments, and at the same time was wonderfully warm and kind. We were terribly attracted to each other and managed to keep it all under control until one night, looking into her dressing room after the show as usual to have a drink and a quick chat about the misfortunes of the evening, she was standing in front of her mirror in her dressing gown. When she saw me she let it slip to the floor. She was beautiful naked, and I was finished. I fell in love with her and she became terribly important to me. Too important: my marriage and family life were threatened, Eve was caused much unhappiness and the affair had to end.

CHAPTER 6

Cleopatra

The following year, 1956, whilst I was filming *Alexander the Great* in Spain with Richard Burton, I was arrested for fishing in the hills outside Madrid. The Battle of Actium was being fought at Manzanares and Richard had told me of a river near the location which was absolutely full of fish. The thought of such sport was irresistible. I had finished filming and should have been on my way home but, as I had my rod with me, I set off with Bill Squire for a few days' fishing.

We came to this brawling mountain stream and sure enough, just as Richard had said, it was packed with fish; every time I put my fly in the water I caught a trout, and dear old Bill, who had never been fishing before, was terribly interested and excited about this. Moving upstream we came upon a notice saying sternly '*Vedada de Pesca*' which I guessed must mean 'Fishing Forbidden'. Pretending we didn't know Spanish, we carried on fishing and were having a thoroughly good time when a man with a rifle popped up from behind the rocks and arrested us. Pointing at the bag over my shoulder, he ordered me to tip the contents on to the ground. Out fell the trout which we were intending to take back to the location and cook. It was all rather alarming as he was very angry, frighteningly waving his rifle about and shouting to us in Spanish, which we really did not understand at all, but we did get the main thrust of the conversation, which was that he was very cross indeed. I managed to encourage him back to the location, where he was mollified by our interpreter and some money changed hands. Apparently, we had been fishing in a breeding stream and what had really incensed him was not so much that we had fished but that we had not thrown the fish back. In the end, we were allowed to keep the trout, cooking them over an open fire.

It's just this kind of adventure that makes filming interesting—that and a good location. Sitting around in a caravan or dressing room, doing the crossword and playing cards, waiting until you might be needed, can be excruciatingly boring, but an interesting location can make up for all the hours of tedium. One of the great advantages of filming is the travelling. The film *Spanish Gardener*, which I made in 1956 and in which I had a large part, is a very faded memory, but I do remember the excitement of southern Spain before it became a tourist attraction and vividly recall the satisfaction of working and living in a foreign country.

A postcard I found the other day, which I sent to Eve in 1961, brings back another moment of happiness when I was on location filming in what was then still known as Yugoslavia:

Have actually left Sarajevo and write this on my knee on the top of a pass just short of Gorazde. I have a loaf of bread, some smoked ham and a bottle of wine and I look down and around at such a view of forest and mountains as I have never seen. Open shirt, gentle breeze, cowbells and not a tourist within miles. I wish I could share this moment with you . . .

How heartbreaking to read and see what is happening to that country now.

For me there is something so unreal about filming that the more surreal the character the more I enjoy myself. I hugely enjoyed *The Bed Sitting Room*, a film directed by Dick Lester from a play by Spike Milligan, which we made in 1969. The names of the characters give an idea of the quality of the film. I played somebody called Bules Martin, Henry Woolf was The Electricity Man for the Whole Nation, Jack Shepherd an Underwater Vicar and Frank Thornton the BBC. A good deal of it was filmed either in a vast field or on top of a dump of broken bits of pottery. Also among the glittering cast were Rita Tushingham, Dandy Nichols, Mona Washbourne, Harry Secombe, Dudley Moore, Ralph Richardson and Marty Feldman playing a nurse (very amusing to watch).

Futtocks End was another surreal film on which I worked, with Ronnie Barker. I played the part of a man who completely changes colour when he eats a hot potato. I was rather proud of that. A film I adored was *The Missionary*, which was set in a huge country house and filmed at Longleat. I was the absent-minded butler who was endlessly getting lost in this enormous palace of a place and constantly showing guests into the broom cupboard or scullery. To go back to my debut on celluloid, however, I first appeared in film in 1939, in *The Girl in the News*, directed by Carol Reed, playing a junior counsel opposite Felix Aylmer. My entire part consisted of me dashing up to him in the foyer of the Old Bailey with the immortal line, 'We are on next, Sir'.

The war had taken up a large slice of people's lives. When it was over there was nostalgia and also a good many stories to tell.

Consequently, a great number of war films were made in 1950s. I found myself in quite a few of them. I have worn the insignia of every rank and rating in the British Navy except that of midshipman, some of it in anger as it were in the war itself—ending up with commander-in-chief in *Sink the Bismarck!*, which was made in a huge model ship in a tank at Pinewood Studios.

In *I Was Monty's Double*, an extraordinary true story about finding a man who was the clone of Field Marshal Montgomery, thus to be able to trick the enemy into thinking Monty was somewhere he wasn't, I played the Governor of Gibraltar. Location work was still something of a novelty, as the hollow studio sound of some of those early films will testify. It was a good time to be in films. The whole industry was alive and expanding. I have made an enormous number of films—many of them sank like the *Bismarck*, without trace—doing things like *El Cid* in Spain with Sam Bronson, an epic film with a cast of thousands which didn't exercise the brain too much beyond the ability to ride a horse. I played Errol Flynn's father in *The Dark Avenger*, Errol playing the Black Prince. Starting in the make-up room at six in the morning, he would drink vast amounts of vodka but never appeared drunk and was always a charming and a commanding presence.

Pacific Destiny, which I also made in 1956, was not a great part in a great film but it was shot in the most wonderful location. The film was adapted from a very popular book of the day called *A Pattern of Islands*, a charming story written by Arthur Grimble, who had been one of the provincial governors of the Pacific island of Samoa. For some reason the film company had retitled it *Pacific Destiny*, a name throbbing with sexual promise and giving quite the wrong idea of the story. (In fact there was rather more sexual promise off the set than there was on it.)

The islands then were not the tourist attraction they are today and we were filming in the island capital. We were a tiny cast of actors, who included Gordon Jackson and Denholm Elliott, and the focus-puller on the camera was Nicholas Roeg, who later became an international film director. We were eagerly awaiting our leading lady, Susan Stephenson, and when she arrived Nicholas and I immediately fell for her. I lost the chase, Nicholas winning the favourite and eventually marrying her.

We were staying in a ropy old hotel called Aggie Grey's Guest House, which was the model for the one in the musical *South Pacific*. Aggie Grey was a half-caste lady of great character who ran the guest house rather like the matron of a boarding school. We were taken under the wing of a Polish chap who was a resident of the guest house, had made it his home and knew a good deal about the island and surrounding waters and took us out 'goggling'. It was an island with a lovely coral lagoon all around it, about four or five feet of deep, warmish water full of sparkling little coloured fish. Clambering over the reef you suddenly found yourself in very deep water and the sparkling little fish were replaced by monsters—sharks and all sorts. The Polish chap instructed us to punch any sharks on the nose and if we met an octopus to turn it inside out. So, trying to remember which was which and not punch the octopus on the nose or try to turn the shark inside out, we swam into the Pacific with our snorkels, following our instructor like ducklings.

At night there were village dances around fires with the Samoans' singing reminding me very much of the marvellous choral singing of the Maoris. When I had a few days off from filming, the Chief of a near-by island invited me to come and spend a few days in his *falle*, a thatched hut built on posts. There were no walls but a system of grass curtains which were let down as protection against the wind, so you were largely living and sleeping in the open air, and very cool and practical it was too. In the morning, the Chief would hold court from his bed and the villagers would come in and sit around him to discuss the business of the day.

There is a creature on the bed of the lagoons of the Pacific Islands called the Pololo Worm which comes to the surface of the water for a few nights each year in some sort of spawning ritual, rather like trout on the Test. On moonlit nights, the villagers catch vast quantities of these wormlike creatures in baskets. I can't remember if they are eaten raw or cooked, but whichever it is they are delicious, better than oysters.

Then I got ill, I remember. I was bitten on the ankle by a dog and, at the local hospital, laughing Samoan nurses fixed up a syringe which they plunged into my backside. It did not work and, leaving the needle where it was, they disappeared for what seemed like several hours, eventually returning with a fresh phial which they screwed into the needle still sitting unhappily in my bottom. Agony. I remember the experience vividly although it was over thirty years ago.

As a young actor starting out in films, I found most film directors very helpful and encouraging, particularly Anthony Kimmins, Fergus McDonnell and Anthony Darnborough. There were only two famous directors with whom I did not get on and who were hopeless at any tactful direction: they were John Huston and Zoltán Korda.

Zoltán Korda was another thing altogether. He needed a whipping boy and, as I was fairly young and new to filming, he chose me, bullying me unmercifully. I found it very difficult to cope with him. In films, theatre or any other medium, I look for directors who can use me and any particular talent I might have, and also lead rather than direct me. 'I'll see what this chap can give me and I'll encourage him' is the sort of attitude I respond to best.

As well as going to interesting locations and earning decent money, you also get to do unusual things in films. In 1967 I was making a film for Dick Lester called *How I Won The War*. He had me doing terrible things in a toga during *A Funny*

Thing Happened On The Way To The Forum. It was always fun working for him and we had lots of laughs during filming. This time he asked me if I could ride. 'Ride? Of course I can ride.' I boasted proudly, 'I used to ride all the time when we lived in Devon.' I had already ridden a horse in *El Cid* six years before so I felt quite confident. What he omitted to tell me was that I should be required to ride a camel. I think he was under the impression that actors are expendable.

Camels don't take kindly to being ridden by amateurs and this one gave me absolute hell. Camels are also remarkably high and remarkably tall. It's a long way to fall off a camel and this one threw me off immediately I got onto it, the camel driver just managing to pull me away from its hooves in the nick of time. Finally, thinking I had mastered it, my director instructed me to take the animal over to a clump of trees and on the command of 'Action' come galloping out towards a group of actors playing a cricket match scene in the middle of the desert, halt, dismount, throw the reins to some minion and get on with the scene. Everything went splendidly as far as the clump of trees, then the camel came to a full stop and refused to budge another inch. A frantic Dick Lester could be seen in the distance, across the desert, jumping up and down and shouting 'Action', but nothing happened. The animal remained rooted to the sand. Eventually, the camel driver, anxious for the future of his camel in films, resorted to drastic measures and rammed a broomstick up the unfortunate animal's backside. This did the trick. We shot across the desert like a bullet out of a gun, with me holding on frantically, at the same trying to look like one who rides camels every day. I am proud to report that we managed the take in one, the camel and I. Thank God I didn't have to do it again. A good camel, I have since found out, is a magnificent beast, obedient, hardworking and priceless beyond rubies. I can only think my camel was an Austin Princess rather than a Rolls-Royce amongst camels.

Probably the most extraordinary piece of film-making in which I had the pleasure to take part happened in Italy in 1962, running on so long that for us actors it became a sort of 'Roman holiday'. It was the epic to end all epics: *Cleopatra*.

We were in Rome shooting scenes in the Forum, colossal scenes, real Cecil B. de Mille stuff with warriors, chariots, elephants and an enormous crowd of Romans being Romans. The days became shorter, the Romans became more and more difficult to control, and then there were the doves. These were supposed to fly out of a huge pyramid which, when trundled into the centre of the Forum, was supposed to open like a flower, spilling hundreds of doves into the sky. Unfortunately, having been incarcerated for so long, they were reluctant to leave their comfortable home and a man had to be employed to get inside the pyramid, which must have been very nasty by that time, and bang about and shout, with the idea that thus encouraged there would be a great fluttering of white feathers and a sky filled with symbolic doves. Eventually, after a good deal of persuasion, the doves trickled miserably out, flying off in all directions only to be found months later, miles away in Naples and Turin.

Each day the sun set earlier and earlier behind the ancient buildings, until it was decided that no more Forum shooting could be done that year. It was madness, the extravagance of all time. By 1962 standards *Cleopatra* was rapidly turning into the most expensive film ever made. There was a definite sense of unease in the boardroom of Twentieth Century Fox. A series of flops at the box office and a feeling that films were going out of fashion as television became the thing made it imperative that this new, highly publicised venture be the success that would restore the flagging film industry.

Fox threw money at it like water. For the actors this meant a long ride on what many feared would be the white elephant of the cinema. One will never know how much was really sunk into the script but I gather the figure crept beyond $40 million. Joe Mankiewicz was expensively extricated from something else and brought in to replace the original director, Rouben Mamoulian. Elizabeth Taylor made her entrance, having negotiated a £1 million contract, which had worked its way up to £3 million by the time the film was finally in the can. As Melvyn Bragg has said in his biography of Richard Burton, 'All was fair in the jungle of Hollywood' and she understood the industry. She would be following in the steps of such greats as Claudette Colbert and Vivien Leigh, who had both taken the role in earlier films of the story. When she walked on to the set, despite the illnesses that often plagued her, she gave the most regal performances. She had an incredible allure and, with those wonderful eyes, it was understandable that she would fascinate Burton, who was deeply susceptible to feminine charms.

Joe Mankiewicz was highly respected and amiably juggled cast and crew, directing us all through the film in spite of some bloody awful weather, and rewriting the script late into the night in a bar or hotel room. Lines would often be handed to you written on bits of scrap paper. This brought a certain spontaneity to the shooting and made for a lively atmosphere on set. Mankiewicz drew a great performance out of Richard Burton, who had lost none of his charm and presence since his Old Vic days. Sadly, though, as three and a half hours were chopped from the final version, most of Richard's finest moments ended up on the cutting-room floor. Joe saw the film as a great epic that would run and run but Fox had different ideas. Perhaps this was a misjudgment on Fox's part, since Richard and Elizabeth's relationship assured a fascinated audience who may just have loved the six-hour epic as much as the three-hour film they were finally offered.

I had been hired to play Cicero. My contract, which had been for eight weeks, was extended and extended until I had finally been in Rome for nine months. Elizabeth seemed to have one illness after another. The weather didn't help. Schedules had to be changed, scenes brought forward, hastily written on the backs of envelopes and filmed the next day, lines having to be learnt on set, which caused Rex Harrison a bit of trouble. There was no question of any in-depth investigation of character; it all had to come off the top of the head, which was all vaguely reminiscent of weekly rep. It wasn't of course to be the last film that we would make together, as I would meet Richard in more portly garb as Henry VIII in *Anne of a Thousand Days*.

Richard's unquestionable star quality was brought out as never before in the role of Antony. He had a tremendous energy that could explode or quietly rumble. It was a great gift and he knew it. Any Roman armour or portly padding was mere cake decoration. You don't need disguises to help talent like that. And the calm of the man, at times this roaring calm that sustained him throughout the long haul. He had a dynamic power that when brought into collision with Elizabeth lit the set. This fusion was tempered by Joe, who seemed to like them both enormously. Melvyn Bragg's biography of Richard is very interesting to me now, as in retrospect it offers an insight into how Joe very successfully disguised his feelings most of the time. 'When you are in a cage with two tigers, you don't let them know that you are terrified.'

Panic, however, was setting in. *Cleopatra* was becoming the most written-about and talked-about motion picture in history. Filming had gone on for so long that the boy employed to play Cleopatra's young son by Caesar had grown too tall and, next to Elizabeth, appeared to be as big as Jack Dempsey. Shooting was continually interrupted for the most ridiculous and unexpected reasons. Rex Harrison made a fuss when he discovered that Elizabeth's chauffeur was getting all his expenses paid by the film company, and refused to continue filming until they accorded his chauffeur the same courtesy.

Then one day in April the loud mewing of a cat brought the entire film to a halt. After intensive searching workmen tore the set apart to discover a cat and four very small kittens cosily curled up just out of reach under the framework of the set. The poor little mother was enticed out with pieces of raw liver, but the kittens took a while longer to extricate and the entire exercise added $17000 to an already straining budget.

But there were some magnificent moments. After endless exhausting work and a further consignment of doves, our earlier problems getting the birds to perform on cue were overcome and the scene that was to form the climax of Cleopatra's grand entrance into Rome finally came together. A blast of noise and masses of extras, dressed as Romans, charge towards the arch of Rome, fifty trumpeters on Arab horses followed by eight chariots dash through the crowd, followed by bowmen shooting arrows with coloured streamers into the air. Dancers flash by, then twelve black men carrying poles from which pours yellow smoke. Behind them six men raise a gold backdrop of sparkling silk butterfly wings. To the sound of drumming, the yellow smoke turns to green and sixteen men in green costumes run at the camera and vault into the air high above the heads of the cameramen. A group of men waving gold fans reveal a moving platform on which are golden temples, obelisks, pyramids, winged girls dancing. Everything is gold. Suddenly, dropping down on one knee, the dancers fold their wings, the monument swings open and thousands of white doves fly towards the sky. Cut to the Forum. Circling overhead, the doves fly through the great arch followed by a mass of people. Camera moves to four hundred slaves pulling a huge black marble sphinx towards the royal box, where Caesar is waiting. A sudden loud silence. Cleopatra steps from the litter, lifts her veil, looks at Caesar—and winks.

In another memorable scene, Cleopatra, dressed as Venus and reclining under a canopy of gold, sailed up the river in a barge with gilded stern and outsize sails of purple, garlanded with flowers. The barge (which is supposed to have cost $277,000 to build) is surrounded by beautiful girls dressed as sea nymphs, some working the ropes and some the rudder. The water around them was thick with swimmers and hundreds of tiny boats, other handmaidens strewing the water with flower petals. There was a good deal of trouble with the handmaidens, who were simply not strong enough to steer the barge. So a hurried call resulted in some slim, strong young Italian men being hurriedly brought in, given costumes and wigs and being positioned on the barge, where they did the actual work whilst the girls wafted around being beautiful props. While all this was going on, the months rolled by and the families of actors and crew flew out to Rome to be reunited with long-lost loved ones. I remember Elizabeth bringing in not only children and a full staff but a menagerie of animals. Eve and Joanna joined me in Rome and we had a merry time. The backers of the film must have been having nightmares, but we all made the best of it and had a very good time at the company's expense. We all went skiing, a very dangerous thing for actors to do, but caution was thrown to the winds, caps flung over windmills and there was a feeling of reckless abandon in the air. There was much socializing and jollity, much taking-over of little tavernas in the mountains.

One evening, after a hard day's shooting, we all took off for a fish restaurant miles away from Rome. Elizabeth came with me in my little car and, neither of us having a very well-developed sense of direction, we drove round and round, stopping occasionally to get out and read signposts by the light of a torch. We became more and more inextricably lost. We laughed a good deal and were rather enjoying ourselves and, I am ashamed to say, we both found it all terribly funny, never giving a thought to any anxiety friends and lovers might be feeling. To everyone's intense irritation, we eventually fetched up at the restaurant, hours late and giggling foolishly, and were greeted by sighs of relief rather than a cheer. Elizabeth being so highly insured, the film company, now tuned for every disaster, had alerted the *Carabinieri* and half the police force in Rome were out looking for us. We felt deeply ashamed.

My old sparring partner Rex Harrison was playing Caesar. We both behaved impeccably, carefully avoiding any reference to the ill-starred *Nina*. But I am sorry to relate that our efforts at civility were rather superficial, and one night in a restaurant, the old hostility surfaced. Having run out of script, we had broken early and gone to have a meal before returning to Rome. Richard and Elizabeth were there with Rex and his wife, Rachel Roberts, to whom he was newly married. I was sitting opposite them with my friend Freda Dowie, who was in the repertory company, and I suppose, what with one thing and another, and probably the demon drink, Rex rather foolishly got on to the subject of *Nina* and was very rude. I was very rude back and I am afraid I leant across the table and struck him rather hard. Our women shushed us and we both calmed down, but it is astonishing to think that seven years later the pain still lingered.

He was a mercurial character, Rex Harrison, and to be fair to him he didn't carry terrible grudges. Perhaps the incident cleared the air a bit. Anyway we spent many jolly evenings after that at his apartment on the Via Appia, and several years later we met in London, by chance outside the Dorchester, and had a very cheerful chat, all old animosity forgotten.

My fishing diary puts it all in proportion:

. . . a good deal to do in the garden at Bagnor after months in Rome on *Cleopatra* or I might have fished a bit more. Paid a visit to the Itchen on a vile day and walked the water. The Main has been dredged and I fear for the future and the weed and the fly and the silt as at Kintbury which is now rapidly silting up and deteriorating after the big dredge two seasons ago.

CHAPTER 7

Working with Pinter, Stoppard and Miller

An adventurous radio director, Nesta Payne, met a lawyer called John Mortimer and, realizing he had a play in him somewhere, she badgered away until he eventually came up with a perfect little jewel in one act called *The Dock Brief*.

A dock brief, for the uninitiated, is a now-extinct legal procedure whereby a criminal with no defence lawyer could point to any barrister wearing a wig and sitting in the court doing nothing, and request that he should represent him. A hurried consultation in the cells would follow, with the unfortunate barrister being paid a guinea from the public funds, and the case would proceed.

I played the clapped out old lawyer whose life had been an almost total disaster, who had never had a case to defend and who was suddenly presented with the defence of an old chap who had killed his wife. It was a hopeless case, but it was the only one he had ever had and he was determined to make the best of it. It was what the *Liverpool Echo* called 'a sympathetic study in failure' and summed up my character as 'a faded barrister, a cousin under the skin to Malvolio'.

David Kossoff played the murderer who keeps insisting on his guilt, the whole thing taking place in a prison cell. We did it on radio and it was a great success. As television had only just begun to impinge on the public, radio drama was still hugely popular (as a little boy said, 'the pictures are better!').

We then did it on the television, with music by Antony Hopkins and with a singing warder. Again it was a great success, gaining for me the Television Actor of the Year Award and inspiring Michael Codron, the theatre producer, to put it on the stage. He was bravely setting up a theatre season at the Lyric, Hammersmith, opening with a play called *The Birthday Party* by an unknown writer called Harold Pinter to which nobody came at all until a magnificent notice from Harold Hobson, who had been to an empty matinée.

As *Dock Brief* was a short play, Codron suggested to John Mortimer that he write a companion piece, or if not, that he might consider putting on a play by Ionesco. Under the impression that Ionesco might be a branch of the United Nations, Mortimer quickly came up with a companion play, an autobiographical piece called *What Shall We Tell Caroline?* about the perils of bringing up a daughter.

So, with Stuart Burge directing and Maurice Denham replacing David Kossoff, who was committed to something else, we opened at the Lyric, Hammersmith, on 9 April 1958 to excellent notices, transferring later to the Garrick Theatre. Its opening coincided with a transport strike, London came to a standstill and plays folded everywhere, including ours. Such are the vagaries of this profession.

49 North Road was becoming too small for us so we went to live in a large Georgian house in Highgate belonging to a friend of ours who had just got a job as headmaster of Dartington, the co-educational school in Devon. He needed someone to take over his London house and we happily obliged, enjoying the unaccustomed space and lovely big garden. We kept dogs, grew vegetables and bought Joanna a grand piano. This piano proved to be an awful bore in later years as, whenever we got the urge to move anywhere, it always had to be considered, rather like some huge awkward member of the family. 'O Gawd, where can we put Joanna's piano?' It was all very worthwhile as she was very good at the piano and when she was nine we sent her to Dunhurst, the prep school for Bedales, where they encouraged her playing.

Eventually, our friends needed their house back and the large Georgian house was replaced by a tiny cottage in Kensington, at the bottom of Church Street. We had got used to having a large garden and although we found our new home convenient we felt cramped and started, in a lackadaisical way, to look for a country cottage, a rural retreat to which we could all escape at weekends. I was by this time a member of the Piscatorial Society, a grand-sounding name for a trout-fishing club which has been a good deal of my life ever since. I used to go down to Berkshire to fish on the River Lambourn, staying in The Three Horseshoes, a pub in a village called Donnington, with a very nice landlord and his wife.

Eve and I were very taken with the area and decided to look around for our country retreat. The local estate agents looked at me pityingly when I mentioned that I might be able to go up to the immense sum of £1,000, disappeared and didn't show us anything until one day, when I was fishing on the Lambourn, Mr Barton of the local agents, Dreweatt Neate, pointed out a row of three Victorian labourers' cottages which were for sale. The cottages were as they had been built in 1870, with solid brick walls but no plumbing—not even a tap—no drainage and earth closets. Water was taken from the river or, if you were very posh, from the tap at the top of the lane. There were also sitting tenants at each of the outer cottages, one being a retired old able seaman who was obviously soon to meet his maker, and a 'salt of the earth', 'diggers of the soil' couple named Robbins. Charlie Robbins worked for the railway and Mrs Robbins worked for anyone in the village who needed some good cleaning done. So we would be buying tenants at both ends with only the middle bit for us. The asking price was £850.

'Each?' I asked.

'No, the whole lot,' they said.

Knowing one was supposed to strike a bargain, I offered £800 and was accepted.

It was 1959 and I was off to New York about this time to do the ill-fated *Moonbirds*, returning six months later to find that the ancient mariner had indeed 'gone to his fathers' and we were left with the Robbins family in the end cottage. Though we explained to them that a good deal of renovating was to take place, nothing would induce them to make a temporary move, so we modernized their cottage around them, and knocked the other two cottages into one. We put in bathrooms and electricity and literally pulled the cottage to pieces around their ears. They put up with it all with great fortitude. When it was finally done, Mrs Robbins was thrilled and excitedly told Eve the comments from their daughter-in-law, Ruby, who had called in to see the renovations. 'You know, mother, it's as good as a council house now.' We felt gratified.

There we have stayed for the next thirty years. I shamefacedly put up the rent to seventeen shillings and six pence and there it stayed until Mrs Robbins followed her husband to Abraham's bosom. Now I rent the cottage to the Watermill Theatre opposite, a project which I viewed with dismay when it first opened thirty years ago since the whole point of moving to the country was to get away from the theatre. But now I have done a complete *volte face* and look upon the theatre and its achievements with great pride and affection, and I am proud to be president of the Friends of the Watermill.

I took a second crack at the Old Vic in 1959, returning to play Pastor Manders in *Ghosts* opposite Flora Robson's Mrs Alving and, directed by John Fernald, Cassius in *Julius Caesar*, about which I can't remember a thing except a terrible notice from the *Sunday Times* which I found in Diana Rigg's funny and levelling book, *No Turn Unstoned*:

> Michael Hordern's Cassius has an anxious air. This Cassius watches John Phillips' alarmingly tall Brutus like an insurance agent estimating how much life cover he can offer without insisting upon a medical examination.

Then there was Macbeth opposite Beatrice Lehmann's Lady M. The press were not kind about this either, saying that I had imposed comedy on Shakespeare and Ibsen where none existed or was intended. I got specially chewed up for Macbeth. In another memorably awful notice one critic maliciously suggested:

> Michael Hordern as Macbeth is ludicrously enough costumed. Half his time on stage he cringed like an Armenian carpet seller in an ankle-length black dressing gown of fuzzy candlewick while his ruched gold cloth sleeves sag like concertinas around the tips of his sleeves. He would make a sinister Shylock, a frightening Fagin. But this Thane of Cawdor would be unnerved by Banquo's valet, never mind Banquo's ghost . . .

It was very funny, very clever, but awfully wicked and cruel.

It irritates me profoundly when actors say they don't read their notices. If they don't they are presumptuous. Second only to good directors I have learnt more from critics than from anyone. Over and over again, I have read something in a notice and thought, 'My God, yes, that hits the nail on the head'.

Macbeth mastered me, but laughter belonged to the doomed hinterland of Ibsen's play. What a night! The audience dissolved into laughter which we may assume was not Ibsen's intention. I submit that if you played Manders today as Ibsen intended you would be laughed at and lose the pity. The only way to take the curse off the situation is to play into the teeth of it and get the laughs deliberately rather than try and fight the audience. The argument of the play is for all time, but the framework which Ibsen gave it and the attitudes themselves are so alien that the audience are going to laugh anyway. I just tried to anticipate their reaction. When *Ghosts* transferred to the West End Donald Wolfit took over. He outlawed any glimmer of amusement and capsized the play.

In 1962 I was in the RSC working in a double bill at the Aldwych Theatre in a brand new translation by Michael Meyer of a short claustrophobic play by Strindberg called *Playing with Fire*, a fearsome affair about a frightful family in which I played a dashing romantic grandpa, and a new play by Harold Pinter, *The Collection*, which was to be co-directed by Peter Hall and Harold himself. Rehearsals took place at the Aldwych Theatre and in a large room at the YMCA in Great Russell Street; I remember we were constantly interrupted as people, presumably lost, stuck their heads round the door, hesitated, apologised and withdrew—to Harold's increasing and all-too-visible annoyance.

Harold had written the piece—a tale of amorous complications and suspected infidelity—for television. I played Harry, a rich middle-aged homosexual dress designer, looking very sly and decadent in a dressing gown. John Ronayne played Bill, Harry's young protégé, with Kenneth Haigh as James and Barbara Murray as Stella. Playing the small part of the maid was a sweet young actress called Patricia England, with whom I fell madly in love, immediately. It was virtually her first job after leaving drama college. She was very funny and very frightened and we made each other laugh a good deal. We adored each other but her heart was elsewhere. Off she went to marry her young actor and live with him in Stratford and have babies. We were to meet again some twelve years later within the hallowed portals of the BBC. The play was Harold Pinter's *No Man's Land*, a radio production with Dirk Bogarde playing the other main role.

But to return to *The Collection*, where did that character Harry come from in my repertory bag? I'm not homosexual and had never played one before, but it was fascinating to find this chap arriving. I got to know him very well and it was enormously satisfying. I used him again later when I played a homosexual man from the ministry in the film *The Spy Who Came In From The Cold* years later with Richard Burton.

I remember we had a terrible time with a cat in the play. We had a double set with my flat on one side and the flat of a woman in the play, Barbara Murray, on the other side. The wretched cat would keep wandering from flat to flat until in exasperation the stage management finally gave it a mild pussycat tranquillizer which had a disastrous effect on the wretched animal's bowels: as poor Barbara was wearing a white suit, the rest may be imagined.

I have worked with Peter Hall two or three times since and I admire him immensely as a director and hugely enjoy working for him in spite of the fact that he once became very cross with me for likening the National Theatre building to

Lubianka Prison—an unfortunate and tactless remark which found its way into the chat column of a daily newspaper. I hope he has forgiven me. I worked again recently with Harold on the radio version of *No Man's Land* opposite Dirk Bogarde and enjoyed that a good deal.

When the run of the Strindberg-Pinter double bill ended in June 1962, I was asked to stay on at the Aldwych, which was the new London home of the Royal Shakespeare Company, to play Ulysses in *Troilus and Cressida*. This was also directed by Peter Hall, with Ian Holm as Troilus and Dorothy Tutin as Cressida. John Barton arranged the fights and Guy Woolfenden composed the music, which was recorded by the RSC's own wind band led by Alec Whittaker. It was an exciting production set in a great round circle of sand like a circus ring. John Nettleton was Agamemnon and Patrick Allen, Roy Dotrice, Ken Wynne, Peter McEnery and myself were his commanders Ajax, Achilles, Nestor and Ulysses. My old friend Christopher Hassall's beautiful daughter Imogen was also in the production.

The following January 1963 I was to play Herbert Georg Beutler in *The Physicists* by Friedrich Dürrenmatt. This was directed by Peter Brook, with whom I was not wholly enamoured. When the three main actors, Cyril Cusack, Alan Webb and myself, used to retire with him to the Opera Tavern for refreshment, after the day's rehearsals were over, I remember he always had a pressing engagement just before it was his turn to buy the drinks. (All rather reminiscent of me and Jack Rayne and the cigarettes all those years before.) Diana Rigg, poor girl, had to lie on the stage for half an hour being dead as the audience filed in and Irene Worth played a very fierce German doctor with an alarming hump. It was a good production and the critic John Russell Taylor thought I played with 'a cool comic flair'. 1965 found me playing Paul Southman again in *Saints Day* fourteen years after playing it at the Arts Theatre. It was only the second production of the play and I had been in them both.

The next year brought work in films, television and radio. After a year of this I was glad to get back to the theatre and a brand new, very funny play by an unknown writer, the young Alan Ayckbourn.

I laughed a good deal at the first read-through of *Relatively Speaking* which was to become Alan's first commercially successful play. It had a small cast—Richard Briers, Jennifer Hillary, Celia Johnson and myself—a complicated plot and was well directed by an irascible Nigel Patrick.

Celia understood the plot straight away but as usual it took me weeks to unravel. Watching me struggling with the vagaries of the plot was, according to Alan's observation, rather like watching a child opening its Christmas present ages after every one else had opened theirs and gone in for dinner. I kept discovering things and gradually began to understand the plot, which involved mistaken identity, deceptions and misunderstanding. It was very clever and very funny. I start the play as a man who is under the impression that he has life under control. He has a young mistress, a wife who cleans the bathtub after him, etc, and all the witty lines at his poor wife's expense. But he gradually has the rug pulled from beneath his feet. He flounders about as his wife, wonderfully played by Celia in that production, gradually gains ascendancy. From being top dog he becomes bottom pussy cat.

In those days, playwrights were always coming up against the censor and Alan had his share of problems with *Relatively Speaking*. There was a lot of worry about plays concerning older men and young girls. How the Lord Chamberlain's mind must have worked. He seemed particularly worried about the implication of sex in the afternoon. He thought that pretty dirty . . . unless the girl stayed overnight! Eventually it was all resolved to everyone's satisfaction and off we went on tour, Celia in her little car and me in mine, and we would fetch up in Newcastle or Edinburgh or wherever it was and have some very jolly times. Touring can be great fun, especially when you are in a play which everyone adores and are greeted in every town by laughter and full houses, and there is always the chance that you might get some decent fishing in on the way between theatres. We stayed at some very comfortable hotels, but one morning, whilst staying in a very smart establishment in Newcastle-upon-Tyne, I had an unfortunate accident with an egg.

Each morning at my smart hotel, I would order two soft-boiled eggs for breakfast, and each morning they would arrive minus the salt. This would fetch up some twenty minutes later, by which time the eggs were cold and nasty. On the third morning of this ritual, no salt as usual, I decided to jump into bed with the eggs, placing them gently between my legs to keep them warm. Preparing for the usual twenty-minute wait, and dozing quietly, I was suddenly woken by a tap at the door. I leapt out of bed . . .

Celia and I had totally differing methods of work. She always knew precisely what she was doing. That is not to say she didn't vary her performance—she certainly did—but she was like a little clock; she always knew exactly where and how whereas I was rather like a man splashing on the paint and hoping for the best. Alan used to come out on tour to have a look at us and one night he remarked that I had lost a good laugh. After a line of Richard's which was supposed to surprise me, I used to walk backwards, shaking and waving my arms around feeling for a chair, which caused a good deal of mirth in the audience. Somehow during the run, this small move had changed to me walking forwards to the chair and that small detail made my situation aggressive instead of bewildering and so the laugh was lost. Interesting that this sort of detail should make such a difference.

By the time we opened in London at the Duke of York's theatre in 1967, we had it as near right as we were going to get it and were rewarded by gales of laughter. Alan was on his way.

After the Ayckbourn I found myself playing George Riley in Tom Stoppard's *Enter a Free Man*, which opened at the St Martin's Theatre in March 1968. It was Tom's first play but the second to be produced. I had already worked on it with Tom for television in 1963 and it came out in November, during the week that President Kennedy was assasinated.

All those years later it transferred to the stage under the direction of Frith Banbury with whom I had no rapport whatsoever and who I unkindly, and probably unjustly, christened Froth Bunbury.

I came across this letter from Tom Stoppard recently.

This letter is about four years late—I blush for the congenital sloth and discourtesy (it's a sort of inefficiency really) that let me omit to write to you at that time to thank you and congratulate you on your TV Riley—it was a portrayal which delighted me and left me filled with admiration for you. You can imagine how thrilled I was to hear that you *had* agreed to do the play for London. That TV was the very first thing I had performed and it made a big difference to my life—I became a little in demand—and I was conscious that I owed a great deal to the warmth, humour and humanity that you brought to the play. As far as I'm concerned, your new acceptance of the role is the best thing that could have happened and I'm looking forward very much to the experience of working with you. I think Megs Jenkins should be perfect too, and I'm very excited about the whole thing.

Thinking back I recall that in 1963 I was very awestruck and thought a note of congratulation from a very new writer would be somewhat superfluous . . . and now I consider myself very lucky to have this second chance to write you an unabashed fan letter . . . Since 1963 you have always been my Riley in my mind.

Thank you!

It was another play about failure. As always with a Stoppard play the talk was good, but, in this case, the plot was fragile and I had a good many problems with it. Opening the play out of London, I stayed with my old friend, Freda Dowie, sitting up late into the night with a bottle of wine and the script between us. She was a great help, her wisdom and good sense getting me through the production. Even so, and maybe Tom would not agree with me, I don't think it quite worked as a stage play. However, it was the basis of a friendship with Tom which has lasted and which, four years later, led to me being offered the part of George Moore in Tom's amazing play, *Jumpers*.

I had got to know Tom quite well and liked him enormously, discovering he was a keen fisherman and sharing a rod with him and his son Dickie on the Hampshire Avon. I was very excited when he sent me his new play, *Jumpers*, and offered me the leading role of George, a preoccupied professor of philosophy. The script was sent to me in 1971, when I was in Belgrade making a film.

My heart sank when I read it. I was being offered this enormous part, I knew the play was brilliant but I did not understand it.

'I don't think I would have written *Jumpers* if I hadn't known I could show it to the National, where they wouldn't recoil from a large play with acrobats,' said Tom Stoppard. Yes, well that was it—a large play with acrobats and as far as I could see my character was a mad anguished philosophy don who was in constant debate with himself whether moral values were absolute or relative: what, in short, is so good about good? In the middle of all this debate he accidentally kills his pet tortoise and hare by shooting an arrow from his bow at the hare and, rushing to look at the carnage, treading on the beloved tortoise. His wife, deliciously played by Diana Rigg, is a pop singer who sings songs about the moon, has the body of a rival philosopher hanging behind her bedroom door and who entertains the university vice-chancellor in her four-poster bed, when suddenly, to confuse even more this surreal plot, a team of yellow-vested acrobats—the jumpers—appear.

Being a bear of very small brain I have occasionally turned down work because I don't understand the script; (to my eternal shame, Peter Hall's production of *Waiting for Godot* was one of these casualties). But sometimes a part comes along which allows you to use all your eccentricities and this, I recognised, was it. Also, I was seduced by the idea that the production was for the National Theatre, temporarily housed in my old haunt, the Old Vic, and that Diana Rigg had already accepted the part of Dotty, George's wife.

Peter Wood, whom I liked and trusted, was to direct *Jumpers*. I had worked for Peter some years before in a play for television by David Rudkin called *The Stone Dance*, playing a revivalist preacher, with Freda Dowie as my daughter, wearing a very fetching flat cap, I remember. Also in the cast were John Hurt and Michael Bryant, who decided amongst themselves that I was the Austin Princess of English actors, an ambiguous compliment which I think they meant kindly and which I wear with some pride.

Peter Wood is a staunch Roman Catholic and had some problems with *Jumpers* having to overcome some doubts about the 'sending-up-of-God' aspect of the play. 'To begin at the beginning, is God?' But eventually, finding the play irresistible, he agreed to direct it and, with this glittering array of talent spread before me, I agreed to play the part of George.

So there I was, in my hotel room in Belgrade, faced with this incomprehensible play, but having a blind faith everything would be all right. In those days there was little to divert the traveller in the evenings in Belgrade, so I sat in my hotel room, stuffing Stoppard words into my head and by the time I returned to London, at least in the long philosophical speeches, I was word perfect.

There were many problems ahead, beginning unpromisingly when Laurence Olivier, who was the director of the National Theatre at that time, finding the play unintelligible, walked out in the middle of the first readthrough. Rehearsals were a hard journey for all of us; it was a densely packed, fascinating play, the first speech, thirteen minutes long, being all about the existence of God! Each day my fists would sink further and further into my cardigan pockets as I tried to make sense of it all. At least with *Lear* there was a period of forty-five minutes when I wasn't on stage and could go back to the dressing room, take off my wig, have a cup of tea and put my feet up before going back on stage for the storm scene. With *Jumpers* I was more or less around for the whole time.

There were unhappy dinners late into the night in Chinese restaurants between Tom, Ken Tynan, who was particularly gloomy about it, and Olivier. It was thought the play was too long for its own good. It was only Tom's second play in the theatre, his first being *The Real Inspector Hound* four years earlier, and he told me some time later that he had got to the stage where he really had no idea if it was all going to be comparatively wonderful or was simply dreadful. The epilogue was cut to half the length and, in a panic, lots of changes were thrown at me at the last minute. I became very cross by that time and shouted a bit, after which they backed down and left me alone to get on with it.

The last dress rehearsal in front of the public was very fraught indeed as the revolve, which was crucial to the play, broke down and had to be mended, making the evening seem interminable. The first night of *Jumpers* was unbelievable, one of the highlights of my career. I had accepted the part on trust and I had been right. The struggle for all of us in rehearsal had been long and hard and when the first laughs came, early on in that first long soliloquy, the relief of finding it accessible to the public was enormous. After that we flew.

Recently, Maureen Lipman, who was understudying the part of Dotty, told me that her husband, Jack Rosenthal, who came to see the play, laughed so much he thought he was going to be seriously ill. The critics were delighted, well mostly. Michael Billington writing in the *Guardian*, said:

Once or twice one of Stoppard's brightly coloured balls falls to the ground, partly because Michael Hordern's moral philosopher substitutes academic mannerism for apprehension of the argument. But this is not to deny that Hordern's simian habit of scratching his left earlobe with his right hand or leaning over his desk as if doing intellectual press-ups is very funny to watch or that he is brilliant at displaying cuckolded curiosity.

Jumpers won the *Evening Standard* Best Play Award which, appropriately, was presented by Professor Sir Alfred (Freddie) Ayer, Wykeham Professor of Logic at Oxford, who I think might have been on Tom's mind at the time he was writing this masterpiece.

After *Jumpers* had been so highly praised, Harold Hobson wrote:

To fail to enjoy it is not actually a criminal offence but it is a sad evidence of illiteracy.

The National Theatre, which, according to journalists, had been slumbering rather under the burgeoning oak tree of the Royal Shakespeare Theatre, regained some of its former confidence. They had been through 'a bad patch'. Olivier said at the time, 'We have to take risks. This is our job. But risks don't always come off. We were perhaps too ambitious. Now we have to be good boys. We are not really supposed to make money but here we are in the rat race!' We felt very virtuous that our efforts would perhaps help to change the run of bad luck which had been dogging our beautiful new controversial theatre.

Still with the company, I went on in March that year to play John of Gaunt to Ronald Pickup's Richard II, giving, according to Frank Cox, 'a good gruff account of this time-honoured gentleman'.

What a lot of energy I must have had in those days. Looking back, I can't imagine how I did it all, for between all this theatre work I was constantly rushing off to play sometimes quite small parts in films, working in the odd bit of television and of course doing the voice overs. These are nowadays a great source of income to many actors. I have no qualms about doing them—though obviously I would not do anything salacious or uphold a product or an idea I found repugnant— but I am perfectly happy to croon about the joys of washing Baby in a particular brand of soap or sit cheerfully atop a giant tin of soup extolling its virtues. If people are happy to pay me, it's just another part of the business, another part of living and loving as an actor.

L'Etoile in Charlotte Street was Jonathan Miller's clever choice of venue for our first meeting, in 1968—clever because it was the perfect restaurant for me, eminently respectable, with a certain glamour and first-rate food. Jonathan, ever instinctive and sensitive to other people's eccentricities, had realized that I would be nervous about meeting this dangerously bejeaned radical, probably a communist, who might not be a gent and whose satirical view of the world might be far from my own. The lunch was guarded and tentative to begin with but after a good deal of splendid food and wine and Jonathan's wonderful wit, it ended with both of us helpless with laughter. Here began a personal and professional friendship which was to be a great satisfaction to both of us.

It was my first contact with Jonathan Miller and very exciting it was. He was anxious for me to play the part of a professor of philosophy, an agnostic who had no time for the supernatural, in a story for television called *O Whistle and I'll Come to You*. Written by M.R. James from a collection of nineteenth-century ghost stories, *O Whistle* had an alarming effect on the viewing public, frightening the life out of everyone and making a huge impact. It is fairly terrifying on the printed page, but I don't think any of us realized how effective Jonathan Miller's production would turn out to be. It was a startling, original piece of filming with very effective use of cross-cutting, panning, long shots and silence.

Jonathan was very interested in the supernatural, not believing in it but at the same time being very frightened of it and interested in what it is that makes the hair on the back of the neck stand up with terror. Giving the impression of shooting the story very simply, he aimed to create an air of foreboding, silence and the feeling of things lurking beneath the surface, this simplicity making it very effective. It was filmed in Norfolk with no fixed script, and a good deal of improvisation was called for. I had never worked like this before and found it very exciting.

'I think we will go out today and do that picnic lunch on the beach,' he would say. 'Take a sandwich out of the bag and talk to yourself.' The only time I was really stumped was when

Jonathan suggested a scene where I engaged the old Colonel in a conversation about extra-sensory perception. I was terrified. 'I couldn't possibly talk to him about anything like that,' I said. So, although it was already quite late at night, by the next morning he had written a long speech on the subject for me. He wanted to make the professor into this eccentric philosopher, and obviously had much experience of eccentric philosophers since he was familiar with the manners, mutterings and murmurings of such people, explaining to me about long hours spent poring over books in the London Library and of the life of Academia which was alien to me for, as I have explained to Jonathan on more than one occasion, I am a bear of very little brain.

This was my first experience of working with Jonathan Miller and luckily for me it was not to be my last, as the following year, 1969, he again took me out to lunch and asked me whether I would play Lear for him at the Nottingham Playhouse.

Lear was not something I had been planning to do all my life but this is not a part that is offered every day of the week, and if someone comes up and asks, 'Do you want to play Lear?' you don't ask questions. I accepted immediately. We then got on with enjoying our meal and spoke no more about it.

I had complete confidence in Jonathan and put myself totally in his hands. He produced the intellectual fuel for me to run on although we didn't have any in depth discussions about it beforehand. He did come down to Bagnor for an evening but we didn't go into Lear in great detail. However, I realized as we began rehearsals that he had the most amazing grasp of the play. Being not only a doctor but deeply versed in psychiatry, he was able to explain the whole geriatric aspect of the character and he wanted me to play him very mad indeed. As Jonathan said in rehearsals, 'It's a very ugly thing, madness— there is nothing pretty or poetic about it.'

Working on Lear with Jonathan was one of the most exhilarating and funny experiences I have had in the theatre. His view was that, if you didn't approach it as a funny play about people going gaga, you missed a dimension and all you got at the end of the day was rather a depressing tragedy about madness and old age. You can't keep your intellect at a desperately elevated level all the time and we laughed a good deal, at the same time working terribly well together. My having my feet on the ground was something he could use, while his intellect was something I could use. He is one of those directors who will take what you give him and use it.

The best thing I remember about Jonathan was his spontaneity, using improvisation though always with a clear end in sight. Moving as much as he does between arts and science makes him immensely open-minded as a director. He never dictates and like Tyrone Guthrie he is very innovative and fresh, taking what you can give him and using it if it is any good.

I was very lucky to have Frank Middlemass playing the Fool in all three of our *Lears* (after Nottingham we did it twice for television). It was Jonathan's idea to have the Fool as a contemporary of Lear. He saw them as mirror images; despite the fact that one had been brought up in the palace and the other in the stables, they had obviously developed an extremely close relationship over the years. But casting Frank, who was roughly the same age as me, as the Fool, was a very bold stroke. He is often referred to as 'boy' in the text and had always been played as precisely that, usually waving a balloon about on a stick. But 'boy' of course used to be applied to servants whatever their age, and Lear and his Fool must go back a long way together.

The staging at Nottingham was very bare, almost Brechtian. When Jonathan directed it again for television it was equally bleak, concentrating on the familial relationship, seeing the play essentially as a family drama and consequently doing a lot of work on the interplay between the characters.

The last two Lears I played for Jonathan (on television) built on the foundation of the Nottingham stage production because the initial interpretation of the play was so strong. But we got better at it each time and the final *Lear* for the BBC in 1982, which is now on video, was undoubtedly the fullest. Learning from one production to the next as I grew older myself, my understanding of Lear deepened. It's not that one respects the wisdom of old age, I don't, but there is a freedom in the old, a basic awareness of human frailty and the passage of time, a state between wakefulness and dreaming, and a speculative reverie between the two states all mixed up in the brain. I feel it myself now. Jonathan displayed such incisive understanding of an old man's state of mind, seeing Lear in a very human and sympathetic light and bringing out a lot of humour which surrounds him, unkind, ironic humour, but there nevertheless particularly in his scenes with the Fool. Irving Wardle, reviewing *King Lear* in *The Times* in November 1969, described this very well.

Lears are called upon to define themselves in the opening scene with the line: 'Come not between the dragon and his wrath'. They can either accept the challenge (as Wolfit did) by belching fire, and carrying on from there as dragons; or they can refuse it and adopt some less resplendent beast. Mr Hordern refuses it, delivering the line testily after a gracelessly hurried, flat-footed entry; an unlikeable rodent figure, whiskers suspiciously twitching. His Lear is a sharp, peremptory pedant; more a law-giver than a soldier, and (as justice is an old man's profession) still in the prime of life.

Far from decayed, and governed more by thought than by feeling, it takes a long time for him to crack. Mr Hordern is not an actor who loses himself in surging rhetoric; and it seems that his Lear is watching and calamities fall as if upon some other victim. So there is no *hysterica passio*, no climbing sorrow, and it is a huge gap;

he scrambles through the thunderous storm speech, and even delivers the curse on Goneril in the style of an icy legal sentence. But the reading is absolutely consistent. 'Fool, I shall go mad,' he says, calmly stating it as a fact; and when, sitting in the hovel with Edgar, he asks what there is in nature that causes hard hearts, it is still in the manner of a trial judge calling for pathological evidence.

He fully enters the present and into the domain of direct feeling, only at the end—carrying Cordelia's body and delivering the final speech in a paroxysm of rage ('Pray you undo this button' is a desperate cry for breath) far removed from the usual elegiac coda. Lear's tragedy in this case is that of awakening to reality only at the point of death; and it emerges as a tragedy of considerable magnitude.

I must have matured in the part for when the production transferred from Nottingham to the Old Vic in February 1969, where Martin Esslin wrote:

Michael Hordern's king is a magnificent creation: there is a nervous fussiness in the opening scenes which explains the antagonism this old man arouses in his daughters, but this expands and unfolds its tragic madness: Hordern's timing of the silences from which snatches of demented wisdom emerge is masterly and illuminates the subterranean processes of his derangement.

One night in 1968, before I had begun rehearsals for *Lear*, I was appearing in Peter Hall's production of Albee's *A Delicate Balance* at the Aldwych Theatre. John Gielgud came round to my dressing room one night after the show; I asked him if he had any advice or help which might get me through the run of *Lear*.

'Yes,' he replied, 'get yourself a small Cordelia.'

CHAPTER 8

Gone Fishing

The decadent, hypocritical judge in Howard Barker's play *Stripwell*, which I played at the Royal Court in 1975, was a bit too close to my own personality for comfort. *Plays and Players* found it muddled and unsure of what it was supposed to be doing but, playing a man wracked by guilt, full of self-doubt and pessimism, I think that for me it was rather therapeutic. Eve and I were going through what is called a bumpy patch in our marriage. A long-suffering woman, she had finally put her foot down. I had been banished from the marital home, which by now was a small house with a dear little garden, goldfish and fountain—and also peace. (One of the goldfish was a savage brute. He ate the others and we took him to the Serpentine. I wonder how many fish he ate there!)

I found myself living in a tiny flat just off Sloane Square, kindly lent to me by Michael Wilding and absolutely jammed with furniture. I do a good deal of talking to myself when I am alone—lots of small noises and grunts, ums and aahs—which is claimed to be the first sign of madness. I remember there was a very unpleasant upstairs neighbour who obviously *was* mad, constantly banging on the floor.

Luckily this unhappy situation came to an end. Eve forgave me my sins and after a decent interval allowed me to come home. Thus I look back on *Stripwell* with mixed feelings, although the critics were fairly kind to me. 'Stripwell's ambiguities are therefore viewed half affectionately and half contemptuously and this comes over well in Michael Hordern's portrayal of bumbling, sometimes endearing ineffectiveness, as skillful and accomplished a performance as one would expect from this actor.'

One of the great things about actors of a certain age is that if you can still stand up and remember your words you are much better value than a younger man with lines on his face. I didn't have to think twice when, in 1976, Trevor Nunn asked me to have another go at *The Tempest* at Stratford, a few hundred yards from the bones of Shakespeare.

Eve and I had had such a happy country summer at Stratford twenty years before—days on the river, picnics, fishing, Joanna playing with her friends in the garden—and we anticipated a repeat performance. This time, we found ourselves a rather grand, bright, airy flat overlooking the river, opposite the theatre in a part of the town called Waterside, and settled in nicely for the summer. I looked forward eagerly to confronting Prospero again.

The Tempest was to be directed by Clifford Williams, with whom I soon realized I had very little rapport, finding him very hard work indeed. David Suchet was a splendid Caliban, covered in green make-up, and Ian Charleson's Ariel was a joy; his haunting singing of Guy Woolfenden's adaptation of *Come Unto These Yellow Sands* I shall never forget. But it was not the happy experience I had anticipated. The designer, Ralph Koltai, who had seen me striding around in rehearsal wearing a long cloak and brandishing a broomstick which was a very important prop to me, appeared at the dress rehearsal with a tiny little baton arrangement and a cloak so encrusted with decoration that when I put it over my shoulders I sank to the floor. I am not good at making a fuss but, after some discussion, a decent stick appeared and the decorated nightmare disappeared to be replaced by a plain schoolmasterly cloak. After the first night, which I can't say was the greatest success of my career but which went down reasonably well, Eve and I were taken out to an awkward, silent dinner by Terry Hands, who had obviously been instructed by Trevor Nunn to look after us.

Don Amado in *Love's Labour's Lost* was a much happier experience and I enjoyed myself thoroughly, teetering about the stage in a very camp, strange pair of shoes with great stacked heels, making the acquaintance of Ruby Wax, who was being an outrageous nymph, and falling madly in love with Zoe Wanamaker, who seemed to enjoy my company but didn't reciprocate my passion.

Stratford was very different this second time around. I was almost the oldest member of the company and, working with a younger generation who had different attitudes and ways of working, I found it difficult. In the 1950s, the company was smaller, more intimate and I was only at Stratford for five or six months. I don't think I am a big company man, finding it difficult to accept the regimes and disciplines of a big company, the notice board, the company meetings and all that, rather like being at school again or finding oneself back in the Navy. I took advantage of the distinguished voice teacher they have at Stratford, Cecily Berry, but otherwise it was not an altogether happy experience. I think I am what one might call a loner, which means I am selfish and egocentric. Very loyal to the play

I am in, but not, as I say, a big company actor . . .

Being at Stratford that season was rather like being on a battleship or an aircraft carrier that doesn't often come into harbour. You are at sea for long periods and away from the rest of your service and if the captain of your ship is a good one then the ship is happy; if not, then the commission you serve is very unhappy because you are a long way from land. At Stratford that season I was a long way from land.

In August 1977 after the second production of *Jumpers*, I at last had the chance to work with Michael Elliott at his magnificent space of a theatre at the Manchester Cotton Exchange. Michael and I had long wanted to work together. I was a huge admirer of his and we understood each other, so I was thrilled when he asked me to play the haunted hero in Ronnie Harwood's adaptation of a novel by Evelyn Waugh, *The Ordeal of Gilbert Pinfold*. It was an autobiographical story in which Waugh charts a nightmare holiday he took on a cruise ship in the 1920s. The play runs for two and a half hours and I was on stage for most of this time, having paranoiac halluci-nations, fighting madness and hearing voices. Michael was an exciting director with whom it was a joy to work. He made the piece into a swirling horror, using increasingly elaborate and terrifying sound effects as my tormentors became more cruel.

Gwen Cherrell, with whom I had worked years before at the Old Vic, was also in the cast and had the imagination to keep a diary during the period of our rehearsals. She kindly gave me a copy and I recently spent a very happy and nostalgic evening rereading it and reliving my struggle to come to grips with Waugh's Pinfold. It tells something of the fascinating journey we took during the making of the production and vividly illus-trates the work and approach of that brilliant and intuitive director whose untimely death in 1984 has left a huge gap in the theatrical world. He is sadly missed. Gwen kindly gave me

145

permission to include in this autobiography an edited version of her diary as it is a much more vivid account of my work in that production than I could ever manage.

The play was a great success in Manchester, with the famous echo of the Royal Exchange adding to the cheers. We confidently took it to London later, to the Roundhouse, where, sad to say, it was quickly killed off by an appalling winter. However, it remains a performance of which I am particularly proud.

After that deeply disappointing season at Stratford and a certain feeling of deflation after *Gilbert Pinfold's* thwarted reception in London, I was thrilled when Granada Television offered me the chance of taking part in a series about that excellent fisherman and writer Arthur Ransome. To be paid for doing what I most enjoy—fishing! The gods smiled on me again.

The chief concern of the fisherman is to trick the fish out of the river. Fishing allows a man to recapture not only his youth, but the youth of the world. He is not moved by a primitive instinct for slaughter. If he were he would satisfy it better with a hand grenade.

These words of Arthur Ransome, from a series of essays about angling that he wrote in the 1920s for the *Manchester Guardian*, were later published in a book titled *Rod and Line*.

Born in 1884, Ransome had a fascinating and eventful life, being a critic, an expert on folklore, a confidant of Russian revolutionaries (one of whom he married), a war correspondent, the writer of *Swallows and Amazons* and other children's stories and, best of all as far as I am concerned, a learned, practised and witty fisherman.

I set out with my rod and line to try and savour a little of his inspiration. We took off to fish in the same waters as Ransome had known, mostly in the Lake District and some of Britain's loveliest rivers—the Swale, the Hodder, the Dove—with technicians crawling around and hiding behind trees and reeds so as not to disturb the fish. The programme, about being an angler, moved at a gentle pace, with beautiful scenery and fine words. If we caught a fish it was a bonus. There was to be no cheating, no nipping down to the fish shop for a frozen trout. The essays were learnt, so when a suitable incident occurred there was a Ransome quote to fit. The only time we did cheat a bit was during a programme about the difficulties of catching a carp and, of course, that day we caught dozens of them. On one particularly barren fishing day, Steve Hawes, the producer, and the floor manager were forced to sit on the side of the river and bait the stream with maggots. Many of the technicians were fascinated by the sport and became bitten with the fishing bug.

My fishing diary records our achievements over four days in Derbyshire.

April 13–16, Buxton Derbyshire. Up here to do two pilots for Granada Television on Ransome's *Rod and Line*. Fished without let up for four days, first on the Dane at Danebridge, a nice little river with some fairly obliging small trout but hideously overfished. Caught six on the dress rehearsal day up to about 8 o'clock. Director Bruce MacDonald, a non-fisherman, impressed. Next day cold and dismal and a horrid NE wind. A unit of some ten people followed me about hopefully and by the time I finally hooked a little fish, I think it was too dark for the camera. The second location (Fishing in Lilliput) was at the head of Dovedale-Pilsbury—quite beautiful but too early in the year. Leafless trees but I caught a few small

147

trout and a large grayling on camera. Local opinion was that no decent fish can be expected till the mayfly comes. After we left, Buxton was cut off by snow.

Angling has changed very much for the worse since Ransome's day, becoming a competitive sport with too many fishermen chasing too few fish. The really wild fishing which Ransome knew has virtually disappeared. Lightweight carbon-fibre rods and nylon filament line instead of the old gut line he used, being much cheaper and stronger, have made fishing easier.

Attitudes have changed too. Actually catching the fish used to be of secondary interest, what really mattered being the expertise required in presenting exactly the right fly to the fish. These days an enormous amount of people have taken up fishing as a sport and all they seem to want to do is catch the biggest fish possible. I have never caught a big trout, in fact the biggest trout I ever caught was a brownie on the Kennet, weighing just over 3½lbs. Nowadays, stew-fed rainbows are put into reservoirs and fished out weighing 15 lbs or more. This kind of fishing is of no interest to me. One might as well be playing ping pong; so unnatural and so different is it from river fishing. Reservoirs do provide a lot of pleasure, but they give the false impression that weight and numbers rather than a day's involvement are what is important.

The basic attraction of fishing is the hunting instinct, the man going out and bringing back the game to the cave. That must be why there are so few women who fish. Those who do, the Queen Mother and Diana Rigg, for example, tend to be rather good at it. It has been described as 'a palaeolithic life without the spur of palaeolithic hunger'. It is hunting of a very refined nature.

'I caught this lovely trout,' you boast, 'aren't I clever?' You recount the wonderful battle, the tremendous fight that must have lasted ten minutes, in reality it probably lasted only two, as it should, for you are there to get the fish on the bank, taking the shortest possible time about it to 'trick the dinner out of the water'. Fishing is a deceptive activity. People tend to think it is a relaxing business. That you spend most of your time patiently sitting with your feet up. Well maybe, if you sit under a green umbrella by the side of a slow, flowing stream or fling a lug worm off the end of Brighton Pier and wait for the bell to ring on the end of your rod, but fly fishing for trout requires constant awareness that action can be joined at any time. Keyed up, full of tension, with a little bit of stage fright, you cannot relax and think about other things. Fishing wipes your brain clean and you concentrate only on the fish. I have made the experiment of trying to do a fairly simple mental arithmetic sum whilst fishing; it cannot be done, your concentration has to be absolute and after a day of this intense concentration I am whacked.

You get to know trout individually in a river like the Lambourn. They are intelligent in an instinctive sort of way. You get to know the one that lives behind that tussock of grass, and the one that always rises by that rock in the middle of the water. Then there is the one in that eddy which is impossible to catch. You pit your wits against them.

To win the first battle in this war between you and the fish you must give him the fly he really wants. I use the black gnat as often as I use any fly in my box, sometimes tying my own. It's a bonus if you catch a fish on a fly you have tied yourself. One of the proudest achievements was the creation of a fly invented by me in a moment of dire need when materials for a 'pheasant-tailed nymph' were unavailable and I improvised. It was a great success and for some time was listed in that once famous bible of fishing tackle, *The Hardy Catalogue*, under the artful name of 'The Hordern Nymph'. This trout fly sold gratifyingly well for many years and I was very miffed when it

149

was eventually withdrawn from the catalogue. In fact I have often wondered whether the Queen Mother, as a sympathetic fellow-fisherman, might not have suggested my knighthood to soften the blow.

Joanna also had her piscatorial triumphs. In my diary an entry in her childish hand dated 26 July 1954 proudly announces, 'Joanna Hordern 2 trout. first trout clever me'. Joanna and I each caught two that day, which was quite fair, hers to the plaudits of admiring trippers. Joanna was six when she wrote her entry in my Fishing Diary. For all that a box of fly-tying equipment may not seem the perfect birthday present for a little girl, this is what I gave her on her ninth birthday. She tied some very good flies, and invented a particularly gorgeous one with a red wool body and a goldtwist. We christened it Joanna's Fancy, and sent it off to Hardy's, the famous fishing tackle people. So enamoured were they with this beautiful creature that they asked if they might keep it in order to show their members. Sadly, it was never returned.

We fishermen do carry more flies than we need. At any moment we are sure we may need a pale watery dun or a blue-winged olive. In fact, we might do just as well if we stuck with one fly through the season. If you have taken a long time with a fish, you are curious to know what it enjoys eating. So with a marrow scoop you pull out the food and investigate what it had for dinner that day. Then all becomes clear. 'Ah, I should have given him a pale watery, bloody fool'.

The romantic vision of days spent fishing, delicious picnic hampers, wine cooling in a fast-moving stream could not be further from the truth as far as I am concerned. I don't drink alcohol when I am fishing (although I make up for this abstinence afterwards) as it blurs the edge of the enjoyment. I take a flask of tea, and a boiled egg which I often forget to eat and find still in my fishing bag at the end of the day. At home I fry the trout in a little butter and eat it with bread and butter and a nice bottle of cold Chablis. Best of all is to cook the fish on the riverbank by making a fire over a flat stone then scraping off the ashes and cooking the fish on the piping hot stone. I keep a screw of salt in greaseproof paper in my pocket. No knife and fork, fingers only, delicious.

My fishing wardrobe leaves a lot to be desired from a fashionable point of view, tending as I do to wear jeans and an old pair of gym shoes. Not for me the flat caps and trilbys of the Hooray Henry brigade. Flat caps are no earthly use as they don't keep your ears warm; if your ears are cold, your head is cold and if your head is cold, the rest of you is cold. I also dislike the green welly, partly because it is trendy, but mostly because it is too heavy and short and consequently always full of water. Waders are light and airy and good for kneeling in stinging nettles. As for the top half, a favourite old jacket with deep pockets and polaroid glasses under, depending on the weather, a peaked American baseball cap or an ancient tweed pull-on hat. Thus accoutred unconventionally, Shrimp and I were one day angrily ordered off the lovely water of the Itchen, haunted by that great writer on fishing, G. E. M. Skues, until we persuaded the irate and senior member of the Piscatorial Society that we were also members.

But I digress and return somewhat reluctantly here—as I did after fishing Ransome's rivers—to the world of theatre.

1983 was a strange, mixed sort of year. It began with a knighthood, which was a great thrill and a great surprise to us all. Joanna, Eve and I put on our best togs and went to the palace to meet the Queen. Joanna's husband, Fritz, joined us later for a slap-up lunch. Joanna and Fritz had married the previous May at Chelsea Town Hall. We were and are very fond of Fritz, a charming, attractive young man who is the son of Sir Clifford Curzon, the concert pianist. To our great joy, we were not only celebrating my knighthood at that lunch but also Joanna's pregnancy. Our first grandchild, Nicholas, was born on 5 September. Eve and I were very proud.

The rest of the year was mainly taken up for me by being one of the awful Absolutes in *The Rivals* at the National Theatre.

'What do you eat for breakfast?'
'A boiled egg usually.'
'Yes, I thought you looked like a boiled egg man. Would you mind eating a boiled egg in the scene?'

In his review of *The Rivals* Bernard Levin was kind enough to suggest that my egg-eating on stage might be a lesson to all students interested in the theatre as a career. I have always enjoyed eating on stage. All my theatrical life I have enjoyed dinner scenes, sitting round a table timing one's laughs with food and drink and *properly* eating, not just pushing the food around the plate and nibbling. In fact, I think I enjoy eating on stage rather more than I enjoy eating off it, so when Peter Wood suggested the egg-eating in a scene between Sir Anthony Absolute and his son Jack, I jumped at the chance.

Perversely, I was also frightened. I had never played in an eighteenth-century play or worn eighteenth-century costume before. Sheridan is late eighteenth-century, of course, and hasn't got all those airs and graces, but the language is what you might call difficult. I have always been a quick study. I learn quickly, but not Sheridan. The writing is so convoluted, so intricately built that if you make one slip it throws you for the next passage. You can't improvise Sheridan. But I love the English language and in the hands of our best poets and playwrights it is so worth speaking and hearing so, of course, I had to have a go.

It was excitingly cast, with Geraldine McEwan as Mrs

Malaprop; Patrick Ryecart as my son, Jack Absolute; Edward Petherbridge, Faulkland; and an exciting new actress, Fiona Shaw, playing Julia; Tim Curry as Bob Acres and Niall Buggy, Sir Lucius O'Trigger. The hero of Peter Wood's production was, in Michael Billington's words, Bath. His review for the *Guardian* gave such an accurate, clear impression of the production that I really don't feel I can better it:

The hero of Peter Wood's luscious production of *The Rivals* at the Olivier is, appropriately, Bath itself. The crescents, the parades, the abbeys, the surrounding fields are all evoked by John Gunter's wonderfully ingenious set which combines spaciousness and intimacy. At first, it seems to consist of a line of four-storey Georgian houses; but these turn out to be made of detachable bricks which, when reversed, contain all manner of domestic interiors.

In short, Wood and Gunter give you, like Sheridan himself, a portrait of a society. So when we first see Jack Absolute he is in comfortable lodgings crammed with clothes-laden shelves which immediately make a statement about his social role. Likewise, Bob Acres, often played as a rustic booby, is here a country gentleman whom we see being powdered and pomaded at the wigmakers, instructed by a French dancing-master, and kitted out at the tailor's where a young apprentice sits sewing and stitching on an upper-floor.

As in his productions of Congreve and Vanburgh, Mr Wood reminds us that characters exist in a context and that comedy derives from the real world.

All this is particularly appropriate for *The Rivals*, since Sheridan wrote the piece when he was 24 after he had eloped to France with the toast of Bath and fought two duels on his return. But the play is also a direct reflection of the fashion-conscious, sentiment-soaked society: hence the comedy of the bookishly romantic Lydia Languish, who adores her lover when he is a poor Ensign, rebuffs him when he is a wealthy heir. Hence also the satire of the self-torturing Faulkland who perfectly fulfils the definition of love as egoisme à deux.

And it is precisely because this production has a sociologist's eye for detail that each scene and character comes up with luminous freshness. Thus Michael Hordern's Sir Anthony Absolute is no mere stage-father, but a gouty, cello-legged, blue-coated Bath Lear, emitting growls of lechery each time he sees a female servant's bottom, leaving us in no doubt that he fancies Lydia himself ('Such eyes, such eyes') and uttering feverish denunciations of his son as he tucks into his hard-boiled breakfast egg. It is highly comic and at the same time blithely accurate.

By the same token, Geraldine McEwan's Mrs Malaprop is hilarious precisely because she takes language so seriously and searches so hard for *le mot juste*. Fastidious and throaty, she pauses fractionally before each misplaced epithet as if ransacking her private lexicography: it is like seeing a demolition-expert trying to construct a cathedral. My only cavil would be that she hardly qualifies as a 'weatherbeaten old she-dragon' and that, in spurning her at the end, both Acres and Sir Lucius seem oddly myopic.

Patrick Ryecart also makes a dashing Jack Absolute, Niall Buggy's Sir Lucius O'Trigger combines velvety Dublin accent with inordinate hunger for conflict, Edward Petherbridge gets to the heart of the Faulkland crisis by making him a self-destructive neurotic who typically smooths out his beloved's drawing-paper after she has intemperately crunched it.

But the whole production is packed with minute observation of character and brings this most delightful of comedies to life by constantly placing private anguish and joy against the larger canvas of society.

It was during the run of *The Rivals* we heard the sad news that Ralph Richardson had died.

At the end of the show there was always a jolly dance on stage with all of us jigging about, having a lovely time, the audience clapping and cheering. This night, after the usual ten minutes of jollity, it was my task to walk to the front of the stage and make the sad announcement. There was a gasp of shock and I suppose disbelief. Ralph was so much part of theatrical tradition in this country, almost a landmark like the Albert Memorial. The thought of his death was unthinkable. We were all terribly moved. After a minute's silence the audience, who just before had been cheering and clapping, filed silently out of the Olivier Theatre.

I went thoughtfully back to my dressing room. Ralph and I had never been close though we had worked a good deal together. I had always been in awe and rather frightened of him, but I felt very sad at the thought of his demise and was probably musing upon my own mortality when fellow actor Patrick Ryecart came up to me and kindly said a complimentary word about my small speech of regret. I am afraid I heard myself saying, from somewhere a long way away, 'I might get some decent parts now.'

It was also during the run of *The Rivals* that Eve was taken very ill with a brain haemhorrage and had to lie absolutely still in hospital for six weeks. It was a worrying time.

Three years later, in the spring of 1986, I was filming in Berlin when I received an urgent message that Eve had been taken to hospital. She had been discovered unconscious on the floor of our London flat, having had a heart attack. She went into a coma and, on 19 April 1986, Eve died. I couldn't have understood, all those years ago on our honeymoon train to Mein Turog, when I looked at her and thought 'What have I done?' that she would be my *modus vivendi*, to be there to say 'This is a wonderful play, you must do it' or 'You were terrible tonight, what were you thinking of?' When I came home from fishing, she would be there to tell me how clever I was to catch such a splendid fish or to console when I hadn't. She kept me on balance when I was depressed or over-elated and I was so absolutely sure that I would go first that, when she was no longer there, I was devastated. I have been a far from perfect husband and father, I'd shilly-shallied a bit all my life, being totally absorbed in my work and fishing, leaving Eve to cope with all the boring minutiae of real life, which she did beautifully. She had given up work to look after our daughter and our two homes and I am sorry she sacrificed her career for mine.

When she died my life fell apart and I felt aimless and, as there had been a certain amount of infidelity on my part, I was filled with a good deal of remorse and guilt. I won't give a list of all the leading ladies I have been to bed with, but it does happen. Two main players in any piece do become close and it is sometimes inevitable, if there is a mutual attraction, for things to get out of hand and there has to be understanding on both sides. But I am getting my come-uppance because she has left me alone and the curious thing is that, if you have spent all your life trout fishing, as I have done, there really aren't many friends to see you into a happy old age. Now even the fishing has lost some of its charm.

We buried Eve in the churchyard at Winterbourne near our house at Bagnor and planted an elm tree at the foot of her grave. Two months later, Joanna and Fritz had their second child, a girl. They called her Eve.

I fell to pieces when Eve died and I am afraid there was a

good deal of public self-flagellation on my part. In interviews and occasional chat shows I was very sorry for myself indeed and, I must say, I did find it very difficult to cope without her support. Domestically also I was hopeless and things fell apart, gardens were not tended, keys forgotten, things rotted in fridges. I remember on something like *Desert Island Discs* giving my usual self-pitying song about being alone and I happened to mention the terrible difficulties I had ironing shirts. For the next few weeks letters flooded in from ladies anxious for my well-being, offering advice and sometimes even themselves. One lady even sent complicated diagrams showing me exactly how a shirt should be ironed. It was good of them, of course, but I felt unable to accept any of their kind offers.

Eventually, with the help of Joanna and Fritz and the kind friends I managed to get myself back on a bit of an even keel and at least sort out a few practical things like gardens and houses. Rooms were redecorated, my friend Sheila Steafel made me some nice curtains and then Toby Robertson asked me to play William in *You Never Can Tell*.

'Curious how the nerves give out in the afternoon without a cup of tea.'

Somebody once said that *You Never Can Tell* is the closest thing Shaw ever wrote to a Mozart opera, an extravagant claim, but I do think it is a very entertaining play. It was a play I knew well, having played the juvenile lead, Valentine, all those years ago at Bristol when I was young and beautiful. This time I was to play the elderly, wise waiter, William, a marvellous character who is inconspicuously in control of everybody. I went through my usual anguish about whether to take the part or not. It would be my first appearance in London since *The Rivals* in 1983 and I had been turning down offers for the theatre for quite a long time, having neither the will nor the inclination to work. But the part of William was too good to miss and I decided to have a go.

We rehearsed and opened at Theatre Clwyd in Wales, which was lovely. *You Never Can Tell* is a curious play; everyone thinks they know it for the luncheon scene, which is like the handbag scene in *The Importance of Being Earnest*. William is real hell to play as he has to serve four courses to seven people whilst carrying on witty Shavian badinage and never getting a plate wrong. It's like a ballet, but once you get it right it's wonderful and should go beautifully and be very funny and sparkling. We had a splendid cast, Irene Worth playing Mrs Lanfrey Clandon, Frank Middlemass (my Fool of *Lear* days) as Finch McComas, the family solicitor, Michael Denison as Crampton the father, and some very good young people—Terence Wilton, Abigail Cruttenden and Harry Burton and Jenny Quayle as the beautiful daughter, Gloria. It was well cast all round. I had taken medical advice before accepting this new adventure and was told I was in fine shape physically. I leave it to the critics to decide what shape I was in as an actor.

We opened in December 1987 at the Haymarket Theatre, that most beautiful and glamorous of theatres, to very decent reviews, although my wig got a good deal more attention than I felt that it deserved. Said one:

. . . this performance is handicapped by the worst wig on the West End stage since Charlton Heston's . . .

You can see Hordern's darker tufts peeping like impertinent country mice through the stiff, lacquered whiteness of his wedged hedge, his scratch patch. Unlike Heston's, his hair does not have a mind of its own and its entertainment value is therefore limited. It merely sits there all night like a dull, stark and frozen sporran. Off with it, Sir, and a curse on all skinflint theatrical hair restorers.

We had a very respectable run. You always get good and bad audiences though and I have always believed that, no matter how good or bad a play is, you usually run out of intelligent audiences after a certain period of time, people laughing when they shouldn't and keeping quiet when they ought to be laughing. Still, it was fun to do and we all enjoyed ourselves. I was beginning to feel a little happier.

I am not generally keen on accepting a part in a long television series as it can so easily limit any other kind of work you might want to do in the future. Maigret, for instance, which I had been offered some years ago and turned down, almost did for poor Rupert Davies, who of course accepted and then found it difficult to move on to something else once it was over. Although the regular income from television would have been delightful, I am glad now I turned Maigret down. The same goes for Dr Who, although I think that that might have been more in my range. *Paradise Postponed*, which we shot in 1984, was different.

John Mortimer wrote the novel and the filmscript for *Paradise Postponed* almost simultaneously. John is a lively man, humble and funny, a marvellous word spinner. After a splendid meal at the Garrick (notice how many decisions I make after a splendid meal and some decent conversation!), I was delighted when he asked me—quite properly, coming as I do from a long line of clerics—to play the part of the Reverend Simeon Simcox. 'I can remember feeling after the war that everything would be different,' John has said since. 'Heaven and earth had opened for us a classless society. The question I ask is why then have we ended up with the same old rubbish?'

An enormously ambitious saga about the decline of middle-class life after the war, *Paradise Postponed* took almost a year to film (it had a thirty-two-week film schedule) and cost £6 million to make. It was to be shown in eleven episodes.

Centring on the expectations we all had after the war of

creating a New Jerusalem in England's green and pleasant land, this was the sympathetic story of four generations of a middle-class family falling into decline. It was set in and around Rapstone Fanner, a fictional Thames Valley village lovingly created by John, the plot revolving around the will made by the Reverend Simcox, a tireless socialist campaigner who bequeaths his not inconsiderable fortune to a local lad who becomes an obnoxious Tory minister. Unable to believe this apparent denial by his father of everything he had worked for, Simcox's eldest son is moved to probe the family's past, searching for things in closets and skeletons in cupboards which might explain his father's death-bed aberration.

Being a man of prejudice rather than principle, I am not one for causes. I would never march behind a banner, or anything else, and I had very little in common with Simcox. But I felt great empathy with him. I liked his plain, straightforward attitude to life, and his dottiness, the way he hung to his faith in a wicked world with a saintliness verging on the simple. Like most of the characters I find myself playing—judges, school-masters, bewildered professors—Simcox is an eccentric. I enjoy playing characters who are slightly off-centre and I sympathise with them because they are not like other people. As the rector of Rapstone Fanner, Simcox had hoped, along with everybody else in the country, that dole queues and unemployment would become a thing of the past—but Paradise keeps being almost indefinitely postponed. The horrible truth has to be faced and, as one of his sons observes, 'the worst thing about the future is that it is almost exactly like the past'.

Paradise Postponed had a strong cast, David Threlfall playing the obnoxious Tory minister, Richard Vernon, Annette Crosbie, Jill Bennett, Colin Blakely, my friend from Stratford days Zoë Wanamaker, Eleanor David and Paul Shelley and Peter Egan as my sons.

The story begins with my death, which the director Alvin

Rakoff had thoughtfully rescheduled for the latter part of filming, observing that 'it is not good for an actor to face his death so early on'.

We filmed *Paradise Postponed* in a vicarage which belonged to a very rich, monocled sweater manufacturer who was very 'in' with the Conservative Party. The room we used as Simeon's study had been draped with CND banners, busts of Karl Marx and the complete works of Engels. Our sweater manufacturer didn't especially want it spread about that his house was being used for commercial purposes, but I am sorry to say that his reticence rebounded on him as, one evening, when we weren't filming he happened to be entertaining a cabinet minister who, after a visit to the bathroom, happened to stray into this left-wing sanctuary and was much alarmed to note his host's taste in art and literature.

I am concentrating a good deal on television nowadays, generally finding myself playing an old person with other old people. In Kingsley Amis's play *Ending Up*, a depressing tale about a group of people attempting to live amicably together, John Mills and I calculated one day at an idle moment during rehearsals that the combined ages of the older members of the cast, Googie Withers, Lionel Jeffries, Wendy Hiller and ourselves, came to nearly 400 years! The same with *Memento Mori*, a play about old age adapted from the novel by Muriel Spark which has been shown twice on television and won an award. There we all are, octogenarians together, and now I am just about to film *Middlemarch*, adapted from the book by George Eliot, where I play most of my part dying in bed. Still, jolly nice to be able to go on working when you are eighty-one and I must say we all have a good time together comparing symptoms of decrepitude. I enthrall them all with tales of my knee operation, the awful pain, how brave I was, and we swap doctors' phone numbers.

CHAPTER 9

Reflections

I have never regretted receiving no formal drama-school training. It wouldn't have suited me at all. Earnest drama students and seekers after truth would have intimidated me terribly. Dazzled by their sophistication, I would have been terrified of being found out. Being self-taught, learning from other actors and directors, I am bored by the intellectual view of the theatre. Actually, it scares the shit out of me, my view being that an actor should learn the lines without too much cerebral interference. I think that a lot of actors are terribly precious, living in the unimportant enclosed world of theatre, theatre, theatre and this doesn't make them better actors. Plays are about the world, about everybody. Neither am I interested in theories about acting. I love the English language; our best poets and playwrights are so worth speaking and hearing, and when I think of some of the glorious speaking in *Macbeth* or *King Lear* it brings tears to my eyes. You act for all you're worth and this wonderful music comes out, but once you try and intellectualize and make it music it doesn't work. Prospero, Lear, Tennyson are my sleeping pills, I lie in bed reciting them as I fall asleep.

Being a poor script reader, I don't always trust my own judgement, seeking out the opinions of people I love and respect. Sometimes I find myself in real disagreement with the general opinion, but on the whole I am not critical at all and certainly not when I am a member of an audience. If I'm bored I twiddle my thumbs or go home in the interval even when I can't put my finger on what is wrong.

Jumpers is an intellectual play, but each little bit makes sense and there is a justification in every part of a scene. I played in it over two hundred times and I was still saying to myself as I came off stage, 'Oh I *see. That's* what that means.'

In 1990 I was lured back to the stage by what I thought was a very funny adaptation by Keith Waterhouse of a book by Craig Brown. It was a gentle spoof on those slightly precious volumes of letters between intellectuals. I played another distracted academic and Dinsdale Landen, a former pupil, now a thrusting young publisher. Directed by Ned Sherrin, the play opened cheerfully in Bath. Things were cooler at Brighton and in the West End its reception was distinctly cool.

As I write this I am appearing in Pinero's comedy *Trelawny of the Wells* and I am finding that each little part of the play does not have its own being, its own justification. The character I am playing, Sir William Gower, a crusty old Victorian vice-chancellor, is a two-dimensional creature. In fact all the characters are a bit two-dimensional. Styles of acting have changed a good deal since *Trelawny* was written and I think Pinero is accusing Victorian actors of being shallow and posing, acting all the time, and is advocating a new breed of actor whose work is founded on truth rather than artifice. I regret my inability to get my teeth into what he is saying. There are fences on the course that I have failed to negotiate. I can see them and I don't know why I can't take them. I think it is because they are not very well built. I am a part actor not a play actor, my job being to get into the mind of the character even if I don't understand the play as a whole. I didn't altogether understand what John Whiting was getting at in *Saint's Day* and I saw Albee's *A Delicate Balance* not, as some people see it, as a religious play but as a play about contact and friendship and the difficulty of achieving these. With the Albee, we had an ideal working situation, ten weeks' rehearsal and no pressures, so that one could grow with the character. Some of my performances were better than others, some of those I thought were bloody good at the time I now know were fairly disastrous and I think, with the instinctive actor that I am, this must happen. Naturally there are times when you feel tired, depressed, something else is on your mind and, if you're not relying entirely on technique, then your performance will suffer. You are playing on your emotions and if other emotions overlap, your performance will not be the same as on the previous night. When I played Macbeth, each night my performance was different. This also happened with Lear, because these parts lean heavily upon the emotions. Technical things, like starting off the evening on the wrong note and, in attempting to get back into gear, throwing oneself out even more, can build up over the evening and destroy your performance. I think it is sometimes a question of how far outside yourself you are standing and observing yourself acting. You have got to be just that right distance away, watching and correcting yourself. But I enjoy acting enormously and when each performance is over in the evening, I am probably not as critical as I should be and I am certainly not good at taking criticism.

Working in the theatre demands a particular kind of energy. You have to project not only your voice but a whole character, learning as you go in rehearsals then still after the curtain goes up, the process continuing with the audience. Film-making is entirely different. You are likely to have to shoot the last scene first because of the weather or location problems, which can be very tiresome and difficult as you can get no sense of progression. With cinema one has to leap into battle fully armed. From the start of the film the character has to be pinned down like a butterfly on a board. One does not always get this right, of course, sometimes starting at the beginning of shooting a film on a comedic level that cannot be sustained. You get a certain sort of satisfaction in delivering what the director wants of you, but the chances of being emotionally involved are slim. There is seldom any question of all the actors sitting down together as a cast and reading the script. Luckily I have always learnt lines easily, which has been a tremendous help as changes are often thrown at you at very short notice. I would study a script and get to know it very well, but I wouldn't attempt to learn it until I was to be used the next day. Then I'd forget it as soon as a scene was in the can.

I quite like the sound of my voice—I must admit that I find it rather nice, which is why I like radio—but I can't bear what I look like, and that's probably one of the reasons why I don't care so much for film. I don't get great pleasure looking at myself on the screen and I never attend the rushes of my own films unless especially asked to by the director. What I do enjoy about film is the attempt at small perfections, getting every possible value out of a scene, hitting the right mark for the camera, the right sound level. Then you can go home and say, 'I did a good half minute's work today,' a technical achievement. By nature a fidgety, strung-up actor, who finds stillness difficult, I have changed a good deal over the years. I have calmed down, saying more by doing less.

It may simply be an exercise in idleness, but one of the greatest pleasures in acting for me is getting involved in an argument about the character. Rather than sit at home with the script, I can only come to grips with a part in rehearsal, opening my script outside the rehearsal room only in order to learn lines, learning them without intelligence as soon as possible after the first rehearsal, rather as I used to learn lines of poetry for prep when I was at school. The 'much scarred and battered jelly that calls itself a brain' finds this very difficult nowadays and I need to spend far longer on lines, but I had a photographic memory once and found learning lines very easy, preferring to have the book in my head rather than my hands, knowing that I was at the top right-hand page or the bottom left, seeing the pattern of the print in my mind, reading it as I went along, leaving hands, body and eyes free to work with until gradually the photograph fades and the words become reality. I can't work properly until I see the whites of the enemy's eyes, hear the voices of the other actors and imagine the set we'll be working on. My fellow actors would think this an extremely bad habit I have kept from my weekly rep days, preferring to hang onto the book until they really understand what they are talking about. I remember Tim Curry, playing Bob Acres in *The Rivals*, frightened me rather by hanging on to his book almost up until the dress rehearsal, but that was his method and he was none the worse for it.

The ingredients of your performance have to be there working with the subconscious and I do remember leaving the stage after a big scene in *King Lear* or *The Tempest* almost not knowing I had played the part. But generally the discipline of lines and moves, the restrictions of the set, conspire to prevent one from being taken over. I think that an actor should always be conscious of acting, a part of him should always know he is giving a performance, that he is acting, otherwise it is a sort of mental masturbation. Coming into the business comparatively late I have always been completely without ambition or a career plan, except to get the next job and enjoy it. I like freedom of action, and if I were back at school now, with the experience I have behind me, I wouldn't conform, I'd drop out and be a nuisance. The uncertainty of my profession, the wondering what you are going to do next, the variety, is all something I enjoy. I have been very lucky; I've kept in employment, I haven't had to worry too much about the telephone ringing, and at the risk of sounding rather bold, I haven't often backed away from a challenge, but was ready to play any old part that was going. Happy to play Toad one day, Lear the next and Paddington Bear the day after that, especially enjoying comedy. But if you ask, '*Which do you prefer, tragedy or comedy?*', it's a bit like the difference between roast beef and meringue, both delicious in their way, but there is nothing more satisfying than a thousand people sharing their laughter with you.

Apart from the Histories and *The Comedy of Errors*, I have played every one of Shakespeare's plays, many of them leading parts. I think it is a mistake to go back and play a part again; it's always a sadness, like going back to the home of your childhood. So I didn't do any of them again . . . except Lear and Prospero. *The Tempest* is a splendid challenge, a sublime play, and I am sure I will never get to the bottom of it. The character of Prospero has so much appeal. I have found this with several parts I played in Shakespeare, that there is this tremendous father-daughter relationship: Prospero and Miranda, Polonius and Ophelia, Lear and Cordelia, all very warm and tender and real. The love between Miranda and Prospero is very delicate, precious, and if you can get that in the opening scene between them then theatrically it's worth its weight in gold. There is all of Prospero in it, his anger and his rage; it's a very wide-ranging scene and should never be dull although it very often is. I have played Prospero to three Mirandas. Claire Bloom was the first, with an inner chilly tranquility which I found rather unnerving. The second was Pippa Guard, who was lovely. Of the last one at Stratford, I remember very little except that I admired her enormously on the first night when, having come into painful contact with a plaster wave, she arrived on set covered in blood and carried on as if nothing was amiss.

I have also enjoyed recording for radio, though playing Gandalf in JRR Tolkien's *The Lord of the Rings* was a bit of a slog. I particularly enjoy being Paddington, that sophisticated and worldly bear who brings joy and chaos in fairly equal measure wherever he goes. Recently, I worked with David Jason, playing Badger to his Toad in a recording of my favourite book, *The Wind in the Willows*, which I am about to record yet again, this time being the narrator. I shall enjoy that enormously, especially as one doesn't have to learn any lines!

In my view, acting is a hang-up from childhood, changing into funny clothes, dressing up and entering a world of make-believe. Not that this makes it disreputable. On the contrary, I think it is estimable, giving a great deal of pleasure to a great many people. But, apart from being an evening's entertainment, I think it's transitory and unimportant. I don't have much time for it as a profession. Not that I am ashamed of being an actor, I'm just not interested in it. I go to the theatre very little, preferring to do it rather than watch it, I am excited and moved by a good performance, but not theatrically interested in it. Large numbers of people make me nervous and irritable and I do not care for the theatrical life, the almost frantic sociability of theatrical people. The Garrick Club, of which I am a member, used to be a haven for actors, but there are not nearly so many nowadays. I enjoy going there occasionally and, when I find myself lunching at the main table, if there are two actors in the group, there are two more than usual, and if they happen to be actors I know and have worked with it is jolly nice to see them, but I will seldom talk acting with them. Actors are lighthearted, mirthful, fun and good company, but I don't have great empathy with them. I will join them in a play tomorrow, but I don't have great respect for them *en masse*. I don't know why, it's like not enjoying the smell of roses or something.

It may appear curious that someone like myself, who has so little time left, who has reached, as it were, the top of my profession, has so little good to say about it. Maybe if I had had more of a struggle I would be more respectful of it; after all, it's been a satisfactory profession to me. In 1972, I was honoured with the CBE, Exeter and Warwick Universities have been kind enough to give me honorary degrees and I am an Honorary Fellow of Queen Mary College, London. In 1980–81, I shared with Celia Johnson the Royal Television Society programme award for our work in *The History Man*, *You're All Right. How Am I?* and *All's Well that Ends Well*. I was amazed, in a generation of such great classicists, to be honoured with a knighthood in 1983. When the letter came in the post I was desperately embarrassed and still wonder 'why me?' A few days after the announcement, Judi Dench and Michael Williams sent me a box containing a bright red balloon which floated up to the ceiling and for weeks looked down at me saying 'Well Done!' Most recently, in 1988, *Drama* magazine gave me an award for, as they put it, my outstanding contribution to British theatre.

Acting has brought me great joy and a good deal of material comfort and it has brought me into a style of living which isn't me at all. I love the country, and the reality of my life is to be found not so much in front of the footlights as at the side of a river with a rod in my hand. If I hadn't had to earn my living I would never have gone near London. You shouldn't be able to see me for dust and small stones. I would be off fishing.

After all the great parts I have played in my career, Prospero,

Lear, Sir Anthony Absolute, George in *Jumpers*, after the accolades, the CBE, knighthood, honorary degrees, mixing with the great and the good, I was brought down to earth recently by a small boy whom I had noticed having an intense argument with two other small boys outside my phone box. I seemed to be the centre of the discussion. When I stepped out of the box, one of the boys came up to me, looked up earnestly and very politely asked, 'Excuse me, aren't you Paddington?' I felt gratified.

'The Ordeal of Gilbert Pinfold'
A Production Diary

Gwen Cherrell

This diary was kept by Gwen Cherrell during rehearsals for *The Ordeal of Gilbert Pinfold*, a play by Ronald Harwood from the novel by Evelyn Waugh, directed by Michael Elliott. The play opened on 15 September 1977 at the Royal Exchange Theatre, Manchester, and played there until 15 October, transferring to the Roundhouse, London.

INTRODUCTION

In 1954, I worked with Michael Hordern at the Old Vic during the first of Michael Benthall's seasons of the complete first Folio of Shakespeare's plays. At the end of it, he was to play Prospero, a consummation he devoutly wished. On the way to it, I watched him rehearse and give some of the most exciting performances in London.

The scoundrel, Parolles, in All's Well That Ends Well *was fixed for a generation with his reading of the line 'Simply the thing I am shall make me live'; his King John The Un-actable committed lèse-majesté by stealing the play from Richard Burton's Bastard and the company was relishing the prospect of* The Tempest *as much as he was—although by this point in the season it was with some trepidation.*

At that time, the designer reigned supreme and the costumes were to be designed by the distinguished ballet designer, Leslie Hurry, whose costumes, like all ballet designs, were emphatic creations rather than 'clothes'.

Rehearsals for The Tempest *began, and as my own contribution was limited to an appearance in the Masque at the end I was able to watch Michael putting together a lustrous piece of work. The final run-through before the dress rehearsal was unforgettable. On a bare stage, under a working light, dressed in shabby trousers with a buttoned cardigan and a practice cloak from Wardrobe, he magicked the island with nothing more than his talent and Shakespeare's words.*

And nothing more was needed. The beauty of his voice and the art with which he interpreted the great poetry was profoundly moving.

The following day at the dress rehearsal, I watched his first entrance with dismay. Prospero's cloak engulfed him with the rigidity of black glass. Worse, it was decorated all over with crude cabalistic signs, the tent of a fairground necromancer. Somewhere from under that costume, Michael had to retrieve the Prospero he had rehearsed. And the performance he had hoped to give.

Somehow, he did it. His performance was acclaimed and The Vic notched up another success. But only those of us who had seen him on that empty stage conjuring his performance out of air—Prospero's 'thin air'—appreciated how great a triumph it was. If it was nothing more, it was an actor's triumph over one of the hazards of his profession. It could have quenched him. I realised then how much I regretted not having charted the rehearsals.

In 1977, I worked with Michael again. He was preparing to scale another mountain. This time I was there with a pencil. I kept a diary of his work at the Royal Exchange Theatre, Manchester, in The Ordeal of Gilbert Pinfold, *adapted by Ronald Harwood from the novel by Evelyn Waugh. In it, I followed his rehearsals, day by day.*

For the purpose of this book, I have cut the passages which have no direct relevance to Michael—the MH of the diary.

THE DIARY

FIRST WEEK

MONDAY, 15 AUGUST, 1977
A. M.: THE GREEN·ROOM, ROYAL EXCHANGE
THEATRE, MANCHESTER

Amiable chaos in a clutter of clapped-out but comfortable chairs, long everybody-tables, books everywhere on shelves, tables and floor, magazines, newspapers, there are paintings, designs for sets and costumes on the walls, jokey notices, half-finished jigsaws, a teddy bear—it all looks like the Act I set for Bridie's play *It Depends What You Mean*.

The actors wait to be formally introduced to each other. Actors always wait to be introduced to each other on the first day of rehearsals. Is it because shortly we're all going to be catapulted into a hugger-mugger closeness, revealing more of ourselves than people do who only concede the bits that stick out beyond their collars and cuffs?

. . . passengers on a liner, first day out—we eye each other then smile delightedly when we are introduced.

Some people already knew each other from previous jobs, of course, and some were in last season's productions at the Royal Exchange. There's a beginning-of-term air about their reunions.

Michael Elliott comes in with Michael Hordern and Ronald Harwood.

Harwood is dressed rather formally. Hordern, as always, looks as if he's just been knitted.

I shared a year at the Old Vic with MH. He played King John, Parolles, Malvolio, Polonius and Prospero. When he left, I was sorry that I hadn't noted then his meticulous workmanship in the creation of some of the finest performances to have been given during those over-decorated years in the English theatre. This morning his obvious and exuberant glee in the pleasures to come, the bones of the acting to be gnawed, chewed, picked and growled over make me decide to keep tabs on his creation of Waugh's Pinfold.

After the coffee and introductions Elliott leads the new lot out into the Hall to introduce us to the theatre.

I suppose that ought to have read 'introduce the theatre to us' but it really was like being ushered into The Presence. The thing stands there demanding homage. And from Elliott's catalogue of its technology and the idiosyncrasies of its structure, it will be by no means the humblest member of the cast. If we don't watch out it'll out-act us all.

Although the Royal Exchange Building and the Café Bar are open to the public, the theatre itself is closed to them. However, we can't rehearse in it because it is undergoing its annual maintenance. The vast room in which it stands is reverberating to the clamour of men and machinery. Men and machinery prophesying Pinfold.

We go back through the double doors and Elliott leads us up a wide stone staircase and past small offices and dressing rooms which have been re-jigged out of old broker's chambers.

INTO THE REHEARSAL ROOM.

Painted white with tomato red doors. There are black-felted, wall-height baffle boards with separate numerals, one to seven, taped on them. These are positioned to indicate the seven entrance/exit doors of the actual theatre septagon downstairs. Until we can move into the theatre, this spare-boned room will be what you might call the workbench.

As for the tools, well, there's the usual makeshift rehearsal furniture—joblot tables and chairs. But these are handsomely supplemented with several seven-seater benches which look as if they've come from a Nonconformist chapel. Horsehair seats, mahogany backs . . . actually they are original Cotton Exchange furniture and carved on the backs they have the letters MRE.

A couple of card tables in the centre of the room hold the set designs and models made by the designer, Stephen Doncaster.

For lack of table space, his costume designs for the seventeen characters have been laid out on the floor—a sort of people-patterned carpet of Waugh's novel.

We peck about, trying to reconcile Doncaster's trappings with how we'd imagined we'd look . . .

Roger Furse once said that in his long career he had never known an actor look at a costume design and spontaneously thank him. Or acknowledge the amount of time and thought that he himself had put into the character. An actor's first reaction is always one of affront.

. . . the Wardrobe Designs will be discussed after the first reading.

But before we settle down to a pre-prandial chat about the play, Michael Elliott welcomes us to the enterprise.

Elliott's voice is gentle, his body has the elegance of a cranebird—long legs, tufted head with long hair that wisps over each ear.

Elliott: Although the play is about the nightmare world of mental illness and it is the story of a man's nervous breakdown, there is a happy ending. In Waugh's words 'There is a triumph to be celebrated'!

The actors grin at each other—'Hope so'.

Hordern leaps to his feet and rubs his hands together like a boy at a party who can't wait for the action to start.

MH: 'triumph' hopefully, possibly . . . but fun! Definitely fun!

Lunch

P.M. REHEARSAL ROOM

We read the play.

Before we begin, Elliott asks for the Stage Directions, always important but usually ignored by actors, to be read aloud. Harwood nods his approval. His stage directions are Waugh-inspired, sometimes taken directly from the novel, and to have them articulated will give a unity to this first coming-together of his text.

Diana Favell, the young stage manager who had earlier introduced herself so diffidently, reads them with a surprising authority.

Harwood smokes his pipe and listens. Two years' work, endless casting sessions . . . probably none of us is as he'd imagined we'd be. What appears to have been the one certainty - that Michael Hordern is the only actor in England who can create Gilbert Pinfold in the theatre—turns out not to be so.

Alec Guinness was to have played the part.

The actors read, laugh at lines in the text . . . at the sudden wit of an actor's phrasing . . . there is a growing exhilaration as we all begin to realise that Hordern is already in command of the comic essence of the play.

Two hours and a half later RH thanks us all.

He asks to be allowed to make one plea.

RH: Waugh's syntax was superb and he wrote English as well as it has been
        written in the twentieth century. Please make the lines comfortable to
        yourselves rather than bending them. Style is paramount. The style of
        the novel must be translated totally for the work to be realised suc-
        cessfully.

Then like all actors and writers he becks wryly at his anticipatory use of the word 'success'.

Wardrobe Discussion . . .

and actors drift away for measurements to be taken, fittings to be arranged . . .

Tomorrow we start to plot the moves.

TUESDAY, 16 AUGUST
REHEARSAL ROOM

At first glance we could be working on a television production.

Unlike the usual quarto-size, soft-bound theatre playscript, this typescript is stapled foolscap and eighty odd pages are unwieldy in the hand, so most of the actors are using their TV clip-files; we are rehearsing in a room with floor-taped acting areas and a multiplicity of entrances and exits; the furniture and props are all makeshifts; the short scenes leave actors sitting around the perimeter of the room waiting on their next entrances; the size of the castlist—seventeen players . . . all these details give the appearance of our working for the camera's eye.

In point of fact, the play reads and feels theatrical—why?

Think it's because its dynamic is quite different.

On the screen it's the camera that provides the energy—from outside. Here it's the character of Pinfold which is the play's core.

Everything that happens is seen through his eyes and heard through his ears. And this must be recognised and identified by the audience as being so.

When the play opens, its vitality will be galvanised from the inside.

Before we start to plot the moves, Elliott talks about his proposed use of the dialogue.

The dialogue springs from different sources. There is ordinary dialogue spoken by real characters—e.g. Pinfold's wife and the Lychpole neighbours, the ship's passengers and crew and imagined dialogue spoken by these characters when they appear to Pinfold disguised as his tormentors.·

Elliott plans to distinguish these by

a)   using the theatre's electronic technology
b)   placing actors in different areas of the
        building—e.g. on various gallery levels within the auditorium, outside the theatre but within the Concourse of the Exchange. . . .

Therefore he asks us to learn all lines of dialogue, even those which will finally be prerecorded and relayed as voice-overs.

Not only will this help Horden to time his reactions, but it will help Elliot to decide which lines should be prerecorded; which lines should be spoken live onstage, offstage into radio mikes; which lines are to be spoken from amongst the audience . . .

The actors who have already experienced all this *batterie de jeu* nod smugly. Those of us who have never actually popped up among the paying customers before look decidedly glum.

So . . .

Pinfold is sitting at his writing desk on a red leather chair . . . For the purpose of rehearsal, MH is sitting at a kitchen table on a perilous swivel chair (typist 1927 vintage).

On the table are a few handprops—milk jugs representing decanters of sherry, tin cans representing bottles of medicine—the bus tickets and empty shoeboxes of childhood that actors play with and transmute into a sort of reality.

MH leans back and begins to read his opening lines . . . 'The Ordeal of Gilbert Pinfold . . .'

The swivel chair gives a scream and cracks him headlong towards the floor.
To plot one's way through a script is also to note the hazards of the rehearsal props.

The Rehearsal Room at the Exchange is small compared with TV rehearsal rooms.

The stage management crew, Diana and her assistants, John Rae-Smith and Chris Monks, have staked out one corner of the room near the long windows for their table with its bells, gongs, notebooks etc.

Sixteen actors wait in seven 'wings'. Hand luggage, knitting, newspapers, scripts, copies of Waugh's novel are dumped on and around other bits of furniture to be used in following scenes . . .

Willoughby Gray (Dr Drake and 2nd General) has brought his sketchpad and is drawing likenesses of the actors.

Elliott picks his cranelike way around and amongst us all. Circling. Always circling.

MH knows the lines of several of the long speeches already.

But as Mark Twain said of his wife's swearing—he may know the words but he doesn't know the tunes yet.

He likes to go back on a scene several times to cement the moves.

Then back.

Then back again.

There will be no scenery for Pinfold's library. The set will be indicated by the presence of the writing desk standing on a square of carpet.

Elliott: The opening scenes of the play are
                straightforward.

Margaret Inglis and I, both brought up behind a proscenium arch with bits of scenery to hide behind, ponder the meaning of 'straightforward' in the round.

I mean, you know where you are with a proscenium arch because you know where the audience is—it is in front of you. There you are either upstage, down-stage, left, right, or off. Here you enter from a perimeter, through the audience, into the centre . . . this theatre's like Sid Field's golf ball—it's behind all the way round!

Will there be new jargon for these new conditions? Elliott still refers to the centre of the arena as the 'stage'. But our moves are annotated in relation to the props, the furniture and the numbered exit/entrances rather than to P. and O.P.

The Prompt Corner for heaven's sake is out of eyeshot and probably out of earshot as well—on an upper gallery!

It is when the ship scenes begin that we appreciate the fun of working in the round.

The cabin is indicated by a taped rectangle on the floor. In it are mock-ups of cabin furnishings—chair, wooden-frame bunk with a biscuit of mattress on it, and, surprisingly, an actual porcelain washbasin looking foolishly 'real'.

MH asks for time to acquaint himself with it. Having demonstrated its ultimate refinements in Doncaster's immaculate model, Elliott (ME) conducts MH around the floor.

Together they ferret about the mod cons like prospective buyer and seller.

MH: Will the taps actually work?
ME: Yes.
MH: (pointing to the empty air) Will that porthole be practical?
ME: If you want it to be.
MH: Will the doors and walls be solid?
ME: No.
MH: Will there be actual wires and pipes?
ME: Yes. Actual copper pipes.

Which parts of the cabin will be solid and which won't are thrashed out before any more moves can be plotted. Practical details of the audience's lines of sight, etc; in a play which demands the use of the audience's imagination as well as the actor's, what is substantially 'real' has to be very clearly defined.

The roles of the figments of Pinfold's bizarre imaginings have yet to be appointed.

We finish plotting Act I. 'Moves for guidance not for adherence.'

WEDNESDAY, 17 AUGUST REHEARSAL ROOM
A.M.: ACT II: ABOARD SS CALIBAN

Ronald Harwood said that he would consider the play to have been a success if it sent one person back to Waugh's novels. Be glad, RH.

The actors here have all read or are now re-reading not only this novel but several others . . .

FIRST GENERALS SCENE

. . . when Pinfold thinks that a couple of retired major-generals are on board and that he can recruit their help in his perplexity.

Pinfold describes the generals:

You know the sort . . . passed over for active command in '39 but served loyally in offices, done their turn at fire-watching, gone short of whisky and razor blades. Now they can just afford an inexpensive winter cruise every other year . . .

Hordern wants to play it without rancour, almost without emphasis.

What Harwood intended is for Pinfold to be seeking confirmation from Glover that Glover has seen the generals, thereby acknowledging their existence aboard ship.

RH: The accuracy of Waugh's vignette is incidental to the pace of the narra-
tive. Pinfold is searching . . . searching.
MH takes the point.
With relish.
He prowls. Bloodhound. Inspector Bloodhound.

THE CABIN SCENES

Satisfied by now that he knows the geography of Pinfold's quarters, MH asks about his costume changes, which will be made *on stage*. Pinfold's suitcase is unpacked and the dinner suit is to be hung on the valet-stand. Question: won't this obscure the view of some of the audience seated at ground level when MH is lying (as he often does) on his bunk?

Elliott: Yes, it will. But what one section of the audience loses it gains in another and because the action is so fluid, it somehow never feels cheated.

Oh?

MH makes a note to bring a change of clothes to rehearsal so that he can prac-
tise with personal props as soon as possible. Even while he still has his script in his hands, he still likes to work with all his props.

He's lucky, making his costume changes while he's on stage. He can at least dic-
tate his own pace. The *doppelgängers* of Pinfold's imaginings will have to leave the stage through one of the seven exits, peel their clothes off (where?), change, bat around the perimeter to enter through a different door, play the scene, exit, peel that set of clothes off, climb into our previous set of combinations, then dash back on stage again as our (unruffled) alter egos . . . I'm glad MH brought the subject up.

But too soon, too soon for the likes of us. Because until we can time the continuing action we shan't be able to time our quick changes.

Elliott: Don't worry about the changes.

Don't worry?!

P.M.

Real toys. Medicine ball, golf clubs, deck quoits, playing cards . . .

We fool around with these props.

The atmosphere is less formal, more relaxed. We are shaking down into a company.

THURSDAY, 18 AUGUST REHEARSAL ROOM

ACT II : THE LOVE SCENE. PINFOLD AND MARGARET, THE INELUCTABLE VIRGIN.

Through the tall windows of the room, I notice that across the alleyway there are business offices on the same eye-level.
A young man is watching us from behind his desk. He is wearing a dark executive suit, white shirt, club tie.

From inside the 'cabin' MH is gangling bashfully—the middle-aged Pinfold as Enraptured Youth.

He is wearing an extremely dashing shirt (milk chocolate and cream stripes), unpressed trousers that fall into elephantine folds, an old brown woolly pullover that he probably sucked in his pram and a tie which has already been tied and untied fourteen times this morning in an effort to time a line. MH: 'May we go back?'.

Lindsay, the ineluctable virgin, is also a bit of a sartorial sensation.

She is wearing tight blue knee-length jeans, red T-shirt, black jacket tailored sometime in the 1940s, and high-heeled red leather mules. Her long yellow hair is *casque d'or*.

She and MH yearn towards each other . . . they must look an unlikely pair, seen from across the alleyway.

Lindsay moves round the cabin . . . 'I love you, I worship you . . .'.
MH beams narcissistically.
She is about to enter the cabin.

A question from Lindsay about the conventions of the production breaks it.
Question: The cabin is skeletal?
Elliott (ME): Yes. Closed surfaces would obscure the audience's line of sight.

Q: So for the 'actual' scenes, the audience will be asked to imagine that these are solid walls and doors?

ME: Yes.

Q: But Margaret is an illusion—a figment of Pinfold's imagination. Can she walk through the 'walls' of the cabin?

ME :   [Thinks—then] Yes.

Q: So does Lindsay the actress walk straight through the wall in order to show the audience that she is an illusion?

ME :   Ah. That might be making too definite a statement too soon. Do we want the audience to be quite sure yet? Pinfold believes that she is real, so I suppose that she ought to enter by the door . . .
        Try it both ways.

Whichever way is decided, it concerns us all. Until now the real characters—i.e. the crew and passengers of the *Caliban* open doors and avoid obstacles. Shall the spooks then move anywhere?

We all lean forward.

By the nature of the piece and the shape of the room, the rest of the cast are constant spectators.

MH and Lindsay try it both ways. For the next forty-five minutes.

Elliott : This must be one of the most original love scenes ever written. The burden of it being I don't exist but I do love you. If you both agree, I'd like it to be touching and funny.

As written, the scene is spare—only one foolscap page in length. It leads to the imagined-by-Pinfold magnificence of Epithalamium. Sounds of glory . . . anticipation of the nuptials to come . . . music, bridal gown and veil . . . a ravishment to the audience's eyes and ears . . .

Elliott decides that walking through non-existent walls which have already been established in the audience's mind as actually existing will be too muddling for them to accept. The previous convention—that the 'sets' are 'real' and 'solid' will be observed throughout.

A final run at the scene. The actors read it with an absorbed tenderness.

I glance out of the window. The young man is watching us again. He's obviously trying to work out what the scene is about. There's no embracing. There's no overt sensuality, yet here's this bird in the tight jeans and high heels, this shambling infatuated man . . .
He's probably fascinated by their besotted concentration. It's certainly better than his own.

We sit around the room and watch . . . or lean against the baffle-boards, eyes closed, relaxed . . . or run through our lines in our heads, faces disconcertingly animated . . . Some of the men are growing beards and moustaches—they tug their stubbles coaxingly . . .

FRIDAY, 19 AUGUST REHEARSAL ROOM

ACT II

The moves for the whole play have now all been marked. But not set.

The internal economy of the stage management—how, when and where the sets-on-trucks and the props are to be moved in and out will finally decide the actual compass points of entrance and exits.

But within the framework of the narrative and the structure of the arena we know roughly where we shall be.

The written text of Harwood's play on the scripted page bears almost no relation to the sounds and shape of the play in action.

As an illustration,
After Pinfold has been driven almost to suicide by his tormentors and resisted them, there is a speech—an aria—which ends with the words 'you are the villain'. On the written page it looks like a catalogue; it plays like a paean of denunciation.

This afternoon, to move it, MH asks if he may read it and see where its impetus takes him.

He goes back a few lines, script in hand, spectacles on nose, then shambling head down he charges into instant attack. Once out of the cabin he stampedes the surrounding space.

Those of us who are sitting on the perimeter smartly pull in our feet and snatch handbags out of his path.

Having hit top C, to our amazement he carries on from there. Onwards and upwards. The force of Waugh's eloquence and the exhilaration of realizing that he actually knows the lines carry him beyond RH's dialogue. He rambles on and on in a superb cadenza of his own, paraphrased from his difficulties when he first wrestled with the speech several weeks ago and his doubts that he would ever learn it.

Whirling his arms into arabesques and his body into *pliés, fouettés* and choreography as yet uncharted, he finally collapses with the words 'My God, I shall never start that speech like that again. I didn't realize I had so far to go!'

End of first week.

SECOND WEEK

MONDAY, 22 AUGUST
TUESDAY, 23 AUGUST REHEARSAL ROOM

In three days' absence, the army moustaches which Willo and Harry Lockwood West. began to grow last week look as if they belong to them, and the beard of Geoffrey Bateman (Angel)—Waugh: 'He emphasised his primacy by means of a thick neat beard.'—has grown gold and glossy.

ACT I, SCENE ONE: LYCHPOLE

Books down. Words to be scrupulously remembered. Hand props, now that scripts are out of the way, to be played with.

MH is given a pair of stand-in walking sticks—not yet Pinfold's, which will have silver tops and be genuine blackthorns. Having conquered the sadistic swivel-chair, MH sets about taming the sticks.

They refuse to lean where he puts them. Their lolling and rolling and the clatter they make when they fall down disturb his concentration and he dries.

Then laughs: 'Bad actors always blame their props.'

Elliott: Not at all. Realistically Pinfold would have the same problems so let's resolve it. Where would Pinfold put them? Lay them on top of his writing desk.

There they're always to hand and under MH/Pinfold's control.

And to hand and under control is where they have to be. The Lychpole scenes establish Pinfold's heavy drinking, his rheumatism, and his hypochondria.

They involve the actor's taking medicines, finding pill bottles, opening pill bottles, swallowing pills, closing pill bottles, replacing pill bottles, offering sherry, pouring sherry, replacing sherry decanter, drinking sherry, uncorking crème de menthe bottle, mixing sleeping draught with crème de menthe, swallowing the potion, replacing the top of the crème de menthe bottle, putting on and removing his spectacles . . . all this while juggling the walking sticks without which Pinfold cannot move. He also has to remember which of the chairs he is in/ near/ beside at any given point.

He is simultaneously performing prodigious feats of memory: Pinfold's speeches with single-line interruptions are often the length of the foolscap page—single-spaced typing.

Where in each of these speeches to accomplish each of these intricate bits of business can only be found by experimenting.

MH's method of working is to co-ordinate the doing with the saying at the earliest possible moment in rehearsal. 'I must try that again.' And again. And again. And when it feels right . . . once more to fix it.

At this time, the hand props are either makeshift or non-existent, so to fix it, he talks his way through. So the dialogue appears to run:

Pinfold: I was halfway through a novel and I had stopped work in early summer I'm taking the lid off the pill-box—wrong—I'm swigging the medicine—right. The completed chapters no, I'm not, I'm taking the crème de menthe the completed chapters had been typed now the sleeping draught typed and re-written or is it the pills now? . . . retyped and lay in a pills surely? No, the draught, and lay in a drawer of my desk. I was entirely satisfied with them, which is more than I can say of my trying to get the top off this pill bottle. I knew in a general way, never mind, I'll assume I'll have got the top off by now, I knew in a general way what had to be done . . . etc.

Having printed the doing, he turns his attention to interpretation, going back and back and back over it again and again.

The pain in MH's voice when he articulates Pinfold's rheumatic agony is excruciating to listen to. Especially over and over again.

These rehearsals certainly emphasise how much more exhausting it is to rehearse for six hours than to play the two-hours' traffic of the stage.

Except that the nervous tension of performance is probably even more shredding . . .

We stop for a re-charge. MH is a dynamic worker and his lubricant is two-cups-of-tea at regular intervals. He apologises for hogging rehearsal time. Elliott very firm—rehearsals must travel at MH's pace.

We go back. Every time we go back on a scene from the opening, we go back to the ending of the previous one. It's a way of learning the play's chronology. The play covers several months during which Pinfold loses track of time. With so many goings-back over scenes, we are all losing our own sense of sequence as well as of direction. The only point of reference as to where we are in the play is to know which scene came before the one we're doing.

It's also a way of learning where in the arena we are, *vis-à-vis* the seven entrances/exits. So while MH is muttering his stage directions along with his dialogue, the rest of us are sliding into our own lines the number of the exit door we're aiming for.

This confusion is compounded by Elliot's simultaneous announcements of the tricks that the theatre will be playing on us in the meantime.

Thus:

FIRST CABIN SCENE

Pinfold: I'm not very well. I wonder if you could
unpack for me.
Elliott: Light change.
Steward: Dinner seven thirty o'clock sir.
Pinfold: I said, could you unpack for me.
Elliott: Ship's engine noises.
Steward: No, sir, bar not open in port, sir . . . etc, etc.

Pinfold is absent from the stage only twice during the action. The first time is after the Lychpole scenes, before his embarkation on SS *Caliban*. MH is marooned on the Library set, centre stage.

MH: How do I get off?
Elliott: Walk off.
MH: Am I in the light all the way to the exit?
ME: Yes.
MH: Oh. Better not stop acting then.
Time for two-cups-of-tea.

The rest of us also relax. Assuming that we'd go straight on from the Lychpole scenes, fourteen of us had spent the last few minutes pinned to the walls of the rehearsal room ready to embark as passengers and pretending to be invisible as actors.

Realising how cramped we feel, Elliott comforts us—there will be more space everywhere. There's space. Imagine more space. 'Imagine space.' We're already imagining two separate characterisations within the same character, as well as imagining doors, windows, props, costume changes, sprints and dashes, light changes and goodness knows what pyrotechnics the theatre is going to throw at us—now he wants us to imagine space!

I look out of the window across the alleyway. There's space there. The young executive's desk and office walls are bare, the room's almost empty of furniture. He's alone. Talking into a telephone. A real one.

DINING SALOON

Having swept through all his previous lines in the scene—i.e. knowing precisely why Pinfold is saying them—MH has difficulty with the speech beginning 'I happen to know most of the Government Front Bench . . .' Why should Pinfold declaim this speech loudly and strongly when he has just asked his fellow diners to excuse his dull companionship on account of his illness and physical weakness?

Elliott suggests that Pinfold is compensating by suddenly boasting and name-dropping. But its also a physical fact that MH is being crowded by the rest of us—we are all leaning forwards towards him.

Give him air.
MH leans back in his chair and the flow starts again . . .

CABIN SCENE

Eager as ever to marry the saying with the doing, MH decided to time his change out of dinner suit (boiled shirt and all) into deck suit. This he has to do in counterpoint to the music of the foxtrot on the deck and the voices of the tormentors coming, as he thinks, from the water pipes.

Shoes and socks first . . . then the trousers, then the tie . . . ah, there is a problem with the tie. Pinfold wouldn't wear a made-up tie, so the tie—which he will have to tie in the previous scene—must be practical. How will he be able to see the bow he's making in that previous scene when there is no 'solid' looking-glass in the cabin . . .

While this is being thrashed out, MH stands unabashed without his trousers, displaying a neat line in domestic underpants.

The young executive looks across from his bleak office and picks up his pen. 'Shall/shall not see R.E.T.'s next production?'

The difficulty of the bow tie remains unresolved. Sort it out with Wardrobe. They'll invent something.

WEDNESDAY AUGUST 24
ACT II

CABIN SCENE

The tormenting of Pinfold by his own terrors begins in earnest.

The Young People from the deck games of the cruise turn into tormentors acting out his own youthful behaviour.

Ian Hastings (Fosker) asks how detestable Fosker should be played.
Elliott: Totally. He is the young Pinfold. The jokes of
          Waugh's set at Oxford were hideously cruel.

The props in this production are as volatile as the actors. For all the study that MH does on the text back in his digs, he can't do much without the rest of us because (a) so much of his performance is re-action, (b) a good many of the performers are props; The blackthorn has to be placed with care somewhere within the cabin where it can be controlled. Here in the rehearsal room, without even the frame of the cabin walls to lean on, a place has to be ferreted out.

By now the duologues between MH and Elliott are beginning to sound like the monologues that MH speaks in his confirmatory talk-throughs to himself. When the Young People have circled his cabin they run away:
MH: They've run off in that direction, haven't they?
ME: Yes, but you don't know which direction they've run in.
MH: I'd better look in the other direction first. I don't know in which
     direction they'll have run.

When Elliott wants to give directions he waits until the end of a stanza.
He picks his way round the actors quietly and delicately, always circling, and never appearing to take notes. His concentration is as riveted as MH's. Waugh gives Pinfold a line of perfect period slang—refers to his giving an enemy a 'kick on the sit-upon'. No sooner the word than the blow—MH sits smartly on the bare boards of the prop bunk, giving his own backside an almighty crack.
The only two of us who don't wince are MH and Elliott.

Where we make our entrances and exits is now constantly being changed as the narrative takes charge. We've stopped worrying about costume changes. The original plot moves weren't even a blueprint, they were just pegs.

MH stumbles on the long speech beginning 'I must think clearly' after his Oxford tormentors have attacked. Elliott suggests that, in Pinfold's paranoia, he is looking for a villain to blame—that's why he goes for the Captain. It's the clue MH had been looking for. The aria ends with the words 'Then I shall act'. MH adds 'if I can'.

Elliott sure knows how to direct actors—you tell them *why*.

Again the problem of translating the written word into action. Pinfold overhears his tormentors say they've given him a present. Note to the stage management— the gift-wrapped parcel must be constructed so that it is collapsible; so that after Margaret has hidden it inside the cabin and he's looking for it, MH/Pinfold *and* the audience must see that there's nothing there. The stage management blanch a little.

DINING SALOON

One of Pinfold's first aberrations is to 'hear' the black steward in the dining saloon say—loud and clear—'Piss!' quite deliberately. The shock of hearing Waugh literally piss on his own prose at this point is terrific. That and MH's reaction to it makes us all laugh at it every time.
Usually by now in rehearsals while we're still groping for words, the actors have let off a few bluebirds. For some reason, so far, none of this company has. Consequently, when MH lets one rip today, it's such a surprise that we all affect profound shock and horror.

We rehearse the absent technology. In order for MH to know from which direction his tormentors' voices come in the arena, we are placed at intervals around the room. When we get into the theatre we shall actually be standing on the first gallery level (amongst the audience, dear God!).
Which of us will be wearing radio mikes and which of us will speak into off-stage mikes is also decided today. This all seems a long way from Coward's advice to just learn the words and don't bump into the furniture.

And all the while there is the nagging dread that one is actually getting the *acting* wrong!

There is a blimpish scene between two generals, talking about a Spanish plot to seize Gibraltar. It is obviously overheard by Pinfold because the generals exist only in his mind. For some reason not explained, Harwood has directed that Pinfold leaves the stage just before the scene.
His exit causes an eerie hiatus.
It's Pinfold's only exit from the ship. Where does he go when he exits—over the side? MH is delighted of course to have the chance of a breather. Nevertheless . . .
The exit is cut. He remains on stage.

THURSDAY, 25 AUGUST REHEARSAL ROOM
ACT I, RUN-THROUGH

This run is to allow Elliott to see progress so far.
We're to be let off knowing our words. If we need the script read the lines rather than hold up the action.

Needless to say it's the rest of us who go first: MH sails through interrupted only by our lapses. When we dry, MH has to halt his clothes-changing. He stands like a stork, one leg in his trouser one leg out with it tucked up underneath him. When we pick up the lines, he picks up the action.

A run so early in rehearsals gives us all a good idea where the text needs pace. Everywhere!

The rest of the day is spent in going through Elliott's 'shopping list' made during the run.

And going back and back, and back again on scenes.

FRIDAY, 26 AUGUST *THE THEATRE*!
ACT II

Suddenly, we're out of our corsets and we're surrounded by space, air, and—because an entire wall of the septagon has been removed(!)—*noise*. And not only from outside the arena—inside it. There is a shattering echo every-time one speaks. MH looks aghast, as Pinfold might: is there an echo in performance?! The voices of the rest of the company reach him from stalls and gallery levels—it's going to be impossible for him to locate them with this echo.

Elliott assures us all that the only echo in performance occurs only when an actor stands absolutely plumb centre stage, immediately under the lighting gantry. And then only he can hear it. Actors standing even one foot away can't hear it. Which is why we shall find that he has placed none of us on the absolute geometric centre . . . MH sniffs dubiously.

He looks upwards, gets a bead on where he thinks the centre might be and lets go with both barrels:

I'm Gilbert the Filbert, the Knut with the K,
The Pride of Piccadilly
The blasé roué . . .

He recites it all the way through, aiming his voice into the air, lifting his shoulders, twisting, turning, pouncing . . . trying to nab it. Actually he doesn't find it.

ACT II: RUN-THROUGH

Our first chance to practise with the actual entrance and exit doors. We empty ourselves out of the arena and into the Royal Exchange Hall, leaving MH alone in the cabin (just off-) centre stage. He speaks the opening lines of Act II.

Pinfold conquers his demons by playing on them a brilliantly witty trick. He bores them. And what's more he bores them literally to extinction.

He does it by reading *Westward Ho!* to them.

They are horrified. As he reads on and on and on and on, they lose their tempers with him. 'You're mad,' they shriek at him, 'mad, mad, mad!'. We all seize this chance to flirt with the echo. What more flattering or delightful? 'Mad, mad!' we all scream, wallowing in the devastating amount of noise we can make. We blast away, rising to a demonic crescendo, 'mad . . . mad . . .'.

MH meanwhile tries to win his battle but it's one against ten—he sinks under the din.

Elliott: *Pinfold* triumphs, not the demons!
            I suggest you all start loud and then, as Pinfold succeeds, you all diminish.

The whole scene is virtually a sort of vocal arm-wrestling. As such it has to be vocally choreographed—the voices rising and falling, insulting then whining, pleading then abusing . . .

We work on the scene for an hour, at the end of which (two foolscap pages mostly Pinfold) MH is reduced to a croak.
Elliott suggests we leave it.
One point MH would like to have settled before we go our ways for the weekend concerns the remaining scenes of the play.

MH: By the final scene Pinfold has defeated all his demons except three. Will the actors who play Angel, Goneril and Margaret actually be seen by the audience or will they be just voices?

Elliott: Not sure yet. Margaret will definitely be seen.

MH: By Pinfold?

Elliott: No. But she'll be seen by the audience.

MH: Ah. Why?

Elliott: Because she is part of his personality. That's why, even though he may not see her, he can feel her presence.

MH: (croaking): I see.

I wonder if he does.
The miracle is that Elliott does. He seems to have disentangled all the levels of consciousness in the text. And however many times he says 'Try it' or 'I'm not sure yet', one feels that he knows the words *and* the music.

I've never been so aware of the text of a play's being so like an orchestral score.

Some concerto!

MONDAY, 29 AUGUST

A. M.: BACK IN THE REHEARSAL ROOM

Actors reassemble. Beards and moustaches lived-in. Scripts no longer clutched like life-lines . . .

ACT I, SCENE ONE: LYCHPOLE.

Refinements.
Angel BBC sets up the broadcast interview with Pinfold.

Elliott: The microphone wires all over his library would appal Pinfold. And his alarm must be noted by the audience for later reference to the wires in the cabin which transmit his delusions.

How to achieve it.
Should MH trip over them? Tangle his walking stick?
These antics are gleefully rehearsed. Then abandoned.
The best way to clock a point is to let it hang in the air.
They select the line 'Be careful of the wires', stick a silence around it, then crisp up the action that follows it.

As in real life (even making a domestic tape recording), the microphone immediately becomes the star of the show. Where on the desk to place it . . . MH stalks the microphone, feints at it, neck extended, grousing. Pinfold and Angel are natural class enemies (Pinfold: I recognise the snarl of the underdog). Try Angel further down the social scale.
MH curls his lip.

However repugnant the idea of entertaining a BBC interviewer in his own house, once Pinfold gets going, he thoroughly enjoys himself. A chance to show off, to patronise. . .

MH settles back into his chair and begins to spout with an authentic altesse. But then surprisingly he winds down at the end of the final speech when Pinfold dismisses Dickens and Balzac as mere professional tricksters.

Elliott: I think that's a superb bit of Pinfoldism and I think it should be delivered with self-confident *élan*. Crisply. Wittily.

MH: I agree. I simply couldn't remember what I said next so I decided to waffle. Let's do it again.

This time he delivers the speech—crisp and witty—but as if Pinfold intends to go on talking all night. When Geoffrey cuts in with his line MH looks deeply hurt. Elliot delighted. 'Keep it in.'

There is a sudden switch in the text from Pinfold's levity and disdain for Angel to his realizing that he must apologise for hurting Angel's feelings.

MH has difficulty with the lines.

'Ungracious' is the clue.

Elliott: He even apologises with a bad grace.

Having discovered how to play it, MH does a little tap dance. He even checks his lines with Diana on the move. The energy burns all the time. When doing yet another run-through of the interview scene (which was going well) he forgets a line because he's got himself into the wrong position; his reaction is to clout himself an imperial blow on his own forehead.

During the lunch break he takes a catnap.

P.M.: BACK IN THE THEATRE

The cabin set has been constructed (but not yet completed) and the carpenters wheel it into the arena for our inspection.

Where a proscenium set has painted canvas to give the effect of solidity, scale larger than life, this set is constructed from actual materials—the water pipes which run around the cabin are made of copper and the stanchions of the 'walls' are built of solid timbers—scale life size. The set is built on a six-foot-high rostrum on wheels. A nice theatre paradox: what looks real is simulated and what looks skeletal is real.

Good thing the pipes *are* solid. MH gives one a thwack with his stick. It holds.

MH: There isn't a real step there, is there?

Elliott: You mean in a real cabin?

MH: Yes.

Elliott: There is something you have to lift your foot over, a sort of barrier, isn't there? Just act that there's a six-inch high step.

MH: (pointing to the rostrum) There is.

Elliott: Act it anyway.

MH takes a time to acquaint himself with the practicalities of the cabin. He opens and shuts the doors of cupboards, the drawers, gets down and looks under the bed, looks for nooks in which to lodge the dreaded blackthorn, swings on the copper pipes . . .

FIRST CABIN SCENE WITH PROPS

The unpacking of Pinfold's suitcase. This takes far longer than they'd anticipated. Where to stow the items—the contents of the sponge bag, the bottle of pills, potions and medicines, the dinner suit, shirt, tie, shoes, socks, etc—all of which MH will need for his later change into them. So they must be put to hand. After two weeks' fluency with the dialogue, up come the crocodile props to swallow it whole.

For all Ron Emslie's skill in unpacking, there are yawning pauses. MH decides that, to fill them, Pinfold would talk to himself. 'Rather like the old Earl of Bellamys.' (Act II. Pinfold trying to find an explanation for his fellow passengers apparently talking to themselves about him: 'When I first joined Bellamys, there was an old earl who sat alone all day and every day talking loudly to himself. . .' It's one of those narrative cadenzas that MH particularly enjoys and we've all grown rather fond of the Old Earl.)

While he is chuntering to himself one of the cabin's heavy copper pipes not yet firmly welded falls with a crash. It misses MH by inches. His back was towards it and he was concentrating so hard that he continued. If it had hit him it could have split his skull.

At the end of the scene, Pinfold tips the English steward. By the time they've gone back and back on the scene MH has tipped him so many times with his own money that on the final run he's out of change; so Emslie tips *him*.

DECK SCENES: CABIN CENTRE—DECK ALL AROUND

Elliott decides that the sound effects of the ship's engines throbbing should be complemented at one point with the impression of rolling seas.
'Enter passengers rolling. Try it.' We do.
The only thing is we didn't check which way the ship was supposed to be rolling. We all reel about in different directions like Hollywood drunks. MH, for once a spectator, quotes Othello delightedly: 'And let the labouring bark climb hills of seas Olympus-high, and duck again as low. As hell's from Heaven'!

To denote the passing of time, Elliott decides to bring on the Four Young People, crossing the stage. The Four Young Actors: Please, may we *not* be happy and laughing this time? Every other entrance is happy-laughing acting.

Harwood suggested this device to conjure youth and lost laughter in Pinfold's mind. This makes their contribution to the action simplistic and, frankly, for the FYAs, boring.

Elliott acknowledges their point. The ship gives a sudden lurch and it's mal de mer and a rush for the side. This cheers them up no end.

DINING SALOON SCENE: PINFOLD'S FIRST MEETING WITH HIS FELLOW PASSENGERS AT TABLE.

Pinfold's aria beginning 'I happen to know most of the Government Front Bench . . .'

MH   (head in hands): Oh, God! I see this long speech coming like Bechers Brook. I can't believe that a dramatist would have written this particular speech for this particular juncture; it's a novelist's device. As the written speech it's a splendid piece of rodo-montade—here, apologetic, and cribbed and confined by the other five diners so close to him, Pinfold wouldn't say all that.

PAUSE

It's the first time there's been so long a silence between Elliott and MH.
We all wait.
Elliot is sympathetic to MH's difficulties and quietly suggests a way around them.

MH   wants to cut the speech.

ME: No. You have difficulties each time we do this scene. Let's see what we can do to make it comfortable.

MH: Cut it.

ME: No. Play it as if it's spoken to himself. Ignore the others.

MH: mutters and casts a piteous eye at the stage management.

MH: It'll be easier when I have all the props.
             The stage management make busy little notes.

MH   (morosely): I'm not a clever enough actor to mime soup and champagne *and* play this complicated aria at the same time. Especially since I'm convinced it's in the wrong place. I'm not an actor like Larry you know. He's marvellous with props. And make-up. I'm not. I'm no good at all at make-up. And I can't do anything right until I've got used to the props. . .

This catalogue of his own inadequacies has a thoroughly bracing effect on him. The more dire his deficiencies, the brisker he waxes.

The rest of us having put our oars in earlier—'why don't you . . .?' and 'if I were to offer you the bread on that line . . .?'—we all sit back enjoying the sight (and sounds—the moans and grunts and snorts) of him digging himself out.

Having convinced himself that a) he'll never be able to play Pinfold, and b) he'll never be able to play anything, ever again . . . he is now so full of juice that he tears into the scene and pleases everybody, including himself.

Elliott, who had coiled his length on to the top of a small card table, nods contentedly, like the caterpillar in *Alice*.

THIRD WEEK.
TUESDAY, 30 AUGUST REHEARSAL ROOM
A.M.

After the luxury of being in the theatre, we have to re-adjust to the dimensions and confusing topography of the Rehearsal Room again.

TORTURE SCENE, END OF ACT I

This is the first appalling horror to hit Pinfold.

MH, having charted Pinfold's gradual decline into break-down during his academic study of the text, finds that he is becoming increasingly bemused by the practical rehearsals.

Elliott puts in the signposts. On Derrick Branche's first scream, Pinfold instantly identifies with the victim. The pain becomes his own.

During the scene, MH has to remove his dinner jacket, trousers, shoes, socks, etc.

A man is at his most vulnerable when he's without his trousers—try hearing the scream after the trousers are off . . .

MH practises and practises this changing of clothes, while timing his reactions to what Pinfold hears in his own head—lines spoken by other actors.

MH: Where will they actually *be*?

Elliott: Probably up in the lighting gantry, using radio mikes.

Derrick Branche crosses his eyes. Its a helluva climb up to the roof of the theatre. And the climb down will have to be fairly fast too. The torture scene ends Act One. The actors will have to make their way down the ladders and staircases with the houselights on, through the audience on its way to the bars!

The thought makes Branche fluff. The timing goes to hell. MH pulls his trousers back on in order to remove them again. And again. And . . .

(The young executive opposite has given us up by this time.)

FIRST GENERALS SCENE

One of the directional difficulties of this play has been how, and *when*, to indicate to the audience which character is real and which exists only in Pinfold's imaginings.

Throughout rehearsals, when he is not muttering himself through the practical action—audibly noting moves, bits of business, etc., to remind himself of sequence, MH bumbles Pinfold's silent thoughts. As a device for clarifying Pinfold's reactions, it works very well.

Thus, after the general's line 'I think the passengers should be told', MH bumbles 'People should know'.

Excellent.

Keep it in.

Do it again. And again.

They rehearse the scene until it is comfortable. They go back to the previous scene to take a run at it. Disaster! Rehearsed in isolation, the scene had perfectly crystallised the identities and relationships. Trio for woodwinds. But taken in the context of the rest of the piece it's *une autre chose*.

For one thing it opens up a rather nasty can of worms.

If the generals are to be labelled 'figments' because they reply to Pinfold's silent thoughts and MH's audible bumbles, why aren't all the other figments preceded by the bumbles? In which case why doesn't MH just give a reading of the novel and Harwood can go home.

Hmm.

Cut the bumbles.

A lot of rehearsals now is 'working through'. Achieving the right end by the wrong route. (Until the audience gets at us and puts us right.)

Rejecting and selecting.

Reassuring to the actors because what we settle for is probably the best when we've tried everything else.

P.M. FIRST RUN-THROUGH OF THE ENTIRE PLAY

Harwood and two heads of departments, Chris Miles and Michael Williams. Our first audience!

We scramble into action, eager for an airing . . .

At the end of Act One:
(quiet voice) Elliott (ME): Thank you. Cup of tea.

At the end of Act Two:
(quiet voice) ME: Thank you all very much.
Tomorrow Act Two.

The run-through played for nearly three hours.

We are all a little bit blogged.

WEDNESDAY, 31 AUGUST
REHEARSAL ROOM
ACT II

9.45 MH arrives. As he comes through the door his cardigan catches on the door handles. He groans: 'It's The Day.' Bad Day.

He throws down his coat, script, etc. He rubs his hands together and then sniffs the air like a pointer. He says his opening lines of Act Two to himself: 'I feel better tonight than I have done for weeks'.
He says it again, louder, to convince himself.

The actors, thinking that he has started, scuttle to their places. He thinks they're anxious to begin so, before any of us know it, we're into Act Two. Elliott arrives and looks suitably impressed. . .

YOUNG TORMENTORS SCENE

Elliott wants them to raise the undergraduate hell referred to—whip the chairs, slash at the furniture, crack the place apart.
They are being too polite, bantering, teasing, in their baiting. ME wants them to howl with blood lust, they're savages. Their demand for 'Music' raucous not gentle. They have to bring all the pandemonium of the Quad's being ravaged by the Bullingdon to shatter the stillness of the night on shipboard.

Pinfold: I must think clearly. Some of the charges are totally preposterous . . ., etc. MH plays this speech of Pinfold's puzzlement slowly and cautiously.
Elliott suggests that at the end of it he should move out of the cabin swiftly and with purpose. This will heighten the level and lift the tempo for the next scene. Try it. MH tries it. And into the next scene, when Pinfold hears Margaret say, 'Here's our chance to give him our presents'.

> Elliott: Try being arrested by the word 'presents' then mutter 'presents' to yourself.
> MH: I'll try. But I think it'll be difficult to switch moods as quickly as that.

It is. He tries it several times. He solves it by using an old Hordern shift. It's a quality in MH's performances I've often noted. The author's words—always learned with truth and spoken with clarity—seem to flow from an impatience to be on to the next thought.

It doesn't matter that the pace of his delivery is contemplative, even slow—the words always appear to be driven, never dragged.

Searching the cabin for the non-existent parcel, MH talks himself through. 'I'm looking in the cupboard . . . under the bunk . . . behind the door . . .' (we are now back to bare boards and few props). Poor old Pinfold giggling happily in anticipation of his present only to be disappointed . . . Going back on it, MH treats us to a bit of a Grimaldi routine. First he scratches his head, pushing aside his always untidy hair, he ends up with it standing out, Joey-like, in three different directions. Then he decides to look under the bunk, giving us the full glory of the baggy trousers . . .
As he searches his clownish joy diminishes into trembling disappointment—he can't find his present . . .

Standing-dismayed acting. Knees together, feet askew, right arm flung up and over his head, hand clamped over left ear, left hand on hip. His face crockled up into quivering misery . . .
Elliott. Right, girls, that's your cue to come on.

They can't. They're laughing too much at this outrageous display of standing-dismayed *over*-acting.
When he wants to make a point during rehearsal, MH won't stop the action. He just goes on and on until he's over the top. Then he has to stop. This time it's the parcel that's fussing him.
This present, this gift-wrapped parcel, the prop, the actual parcel—where will the girls actually have put it? It's a very small cabin, the number of hiding places are few. At the moment they are acting hiding it under the bunk. MH rolls his eye. 'I can't help but see it'.

    Elliott: Cut the parcel. We don't need a real one.
               It's all in Pinfold's mind.

The stage management lift their pencils: cut the parcel?
Cut the parcel. They strike it off the prop list with undisguised relief. Collapsible parcels they *didn't* need.

They go back on the scene to rehearse the girls *not* having a parcel.

Then they forget where on the deck they are supposed to be.
ME: You can be anywhere. You're figments of his imagination . . .

All that *space* again.

MH: What happens now?
After each scene he looks to Diana in her corner. 'What happens now?'

DINING SALOON BREAKFAST SCENE
The tablelamp. The star turn. It blinks.

Why does it blink? Is it a faulty lightbulb which is transformed by Pinfold's sickness into a manifestation of his tormentors? (It is their voices that Pinfold hears every time the lamp winks.) Or should it only blink when they are actually speaking?

If it's on the blink all the time, the scene loses its comic shock. But if it only blinks when they are speaking to Pinfold, why haven't any previous bits of hardware blinked? He's heard all their voices before, after all.

This takes quite a time to sort out. It's resolved thus: the voices of the actors will emanate from the tablelamp. So MH can address the lamp when he's talking to them.

MH: But the general's voice and Margaret's voice are separate in Pinfold's mind, don't you think? Separate from the voices transmitted through the lamp. It makes it much easier to play, if Pinfold is reacting to two sets of voices coming from two different sources—and much funnier. Because he is answering the steward and (groans—oh, God) spreading toast with butter and marmalade at the same time.

His ears droop at the thought.

Elliott: I know it's all a bit difficult to envisage in the rehearsal room but when we've got the microphones and the recorded voices and all the speakers, and the sound effects of the ship's engines, and the dragging chains and the fog-horns and the dance music and the factory machinery and the nightingales and all the props and trucks, it'll be much easier.

It will?!

DECK SCENE

Silent passenger, Murdoch.

Murdoch looks at Pinfold, looks at his watch and makes a note. This simple and innocent gesture is interpreted by Pinfold as being full of unnerving significance. MH finds this difficult to convey. Neither has any lines and that is the full content of the scene. There is no particular reason for Pinfold to find the encounter so alarming . . .

Elliott decides to feed it.
Going back to Waugh's novel, he inserts some lines into the script, concerning Murdoch and spoken by the Captain.

Captain (voice over): . . . we have an extra man on board. He's not a passenger. He's not one of the crew . . . I daresay you've noticed him sitting alone in the dining saloon. All I've been told is that he's very important to HMG . . .

This to be spoken over the playing of the scene.
It gives Murdoch's look at Pinfold instant significance.
Like adding background music to a movie soundtrack . . ..
MH does virtually nothing but the scene is immediately heightened.

Coming at him as something quite fresh, it comes as a tonic to MH. He's been studying and rehearsing the text for so many weeks—a sudden new flourish to be woven into the fabric is refreshing.

MH's method of learning lines is to give himself mnemonics—vowels. There are two separate lines using words with similar 'au' vowel sounds.

Pinfold: The wiring in this ship is in need of an overhaul.
Pinfold: There must be a fault in the wiring.

This morning he gets them out of sequence and substitutes the second for the first. Diana puts him right.
Several lines further on he has the line, 'I wish to send a telegram. To Pinfold, Lychpole, England.'

With great conviction he delivers it, 'I wish to send a telegram. To Lychpole, Pinfold, England'.
Then he laughs and says, 'My God, talk about vowel sounds!
I wish Waugh had chosen different names for Pinfold and Lychpole—the vowels are a perfect match!'

A tease to an actor, but presumably that's precisely why Waugh did choose the names.

The complete line runs 'I wish to send a telegram. To Pinfold, Lychpole, England. Entirely cured. All love. Gilbert.'

MH has been dictating it to the steward as to a secretary.
All in one. Because of the Lychpole/Pinfold tangle, he decides to go back on it and take a flying leap at the line.

He commands the steward to take the telegram, then suddenly, head flung back, he roars defiantly at his unseen adversaries, 'Entirely Cured!'. Then as a sweetly timed afterthought, he adds in a mumble 'All love. Gilbert'.

And then stumps off. We all applaud. And it's lunch.

Today—so far—is definitely not The Day.

THURSDAY, 1 SEPTEMBER REHEARSAL ROOM
PINFOLD'S 'OLD EARL OF BELLAMYS' SPEECH.

Having set Pinfold's mania that it is the passengers who are afflicted and not himself, MH feels that Pinfold is bewildered by their behaviour. To go into a retrospective soliloquy about the old boy, though a delicious caprice, will be difficult for him as a performer, and for the audience to accept, without losing the thread of the action.

MH: It's going to be difficult for the audience to know whether they should actually laugh at Waugh's pyrotechnics. And if they do—as they should—won't this break the tension of Pinfold's dilemma?

Elliott: What do you suggest?

MH: Leave in the first and last lines of the speech. Cut the middle of the speech and lose the old earl altogether.

(cries of 'shame!' from the rest of us)

This keeps the flow of the narrative. As a speech it's fine but at this point not, alas, worth its place.

THE LOVE SCENE: PINFOLD AND MARGARET

Does MH play Pinfold matter-of-fact: 'Come and have a cocktail with me'? Or is he already enchanted by this delectable creature? Does he enter her world or does she enter his?

Elliott: He enters hers. Out of his dejection comes Margaret. Waugh says of his own experiences he was constantly being surprised by what happened.

Margaret: 'I love you, love you, love you . . .'

Lindsay enjoys wearing second-hand clothes. She stands outside the cabin wearing a pure silk thirties dress with her long hair on her shoulders, looking fragile and vulnerable.

Elliott: Try it circling him.

She tries it.

It isn't right.

Elliott: I know what's wrong. You had a free, seductive air when you first did the scene. Now there's an anxiety—an anxiety's crept in.

L: I meant it to. It's Margaret's anxiety. She wants to please him.

ME: I think that's wrong. The anxieties ultimately have to be Pinfold's. Your anxiety has subtly changed the emphasis. Another thing—will you be wearing those shoes?

L: No.

ME: Take them off. Try barefoot for this scene as well as for the bridal scene.

She takes her shoes off and sways round and round the outside of the cabin, with Pinfold seated inside.

ME(murmurs):   Good . . . good. Don't lose the bloom of the interpretation—keep the bloom . . .

He concentrates on Lindsay, following her around the room. Then he transfers his attention to MH.

In responding to Lindsay's change of emphasis, he has now lost his earlier coyness. He reacts to Margaret as a man not as a boy.

He's sure lost *his* bloom!

He pleads that he's reluctant to play coy for fear of getting the wrong laughs for the scene. Touching *and* funny, not touching *but* funny.

To coax MH back to confidence, Elliott suggests that this is the first time Pinfold doesn't suspect that Margaret's voice is not a fault in the wires. He accepts that he can hear her, that she is there, that she exists.

Elliott: In the book, it's here that Pinfold realizes that he doesn't have to speak aloud to the voices. That he has only to think his replies.

MH: Does 'where are you?' mean not where are you in the ship but where are you in my head?

ME: No. I think this carries Pinfold too far too soon.

ME refers ahead in the text to the final scene of the play. Pinfold says 'You mean I've imagined everything' and Margaret says 'It's true, darling, I don't exist'. It isn't until the end of the play that Pinfold acknowledges that it's all been in his own head.

So Lindsay and MH play the scene, again. She barefoot on the move, wooing him, MH less *exalté*, more charmed and delighted . . .

I reckon they've both got their blooms back.

There is an exchange of dialogue between Margaret and her father on the deck to which Pinfold listens from inside the cabin.

While Lindsay and Harry Lockwood West talk through the scene, MH lies back on the bunk. He suddenly laughs aloud.

MH: One's always discovering new things in this script. The father's line 'Come here, Megs'. Reggie's bitch terrier in Act One is called Meg. And Reggie refers to her as 'sniffing about the stables'. On comes Harry in Act Two addressing his daughter as 'Meg' and calling his wife an old bitch!

MH has a vision of Lindsay as Margaret sniffing about outside the cabin . . .
Goneril and the Furies incite the Roman Catholic Pinfold to take his own life, to
throw himself overboard. From the moment that he resists them he starts to win
the battle for his own sanity.

He denounces Angel—the speech ending with the words 'You are the Villain'.
MH, carried along by the impetus of our raised voices as the driving Furies, con-
tinues full tilt at the speech, ending on a tremendous vocal drum-roll of triumph—
'you are the villain!'

But what he'd forgotten is that he's still got nine more pages of script to play. With
the massive cadenza of *Westward Ho!* ahead.

This hits him just as he reaches 'You are the villain' and he goes on at full throttle
'And I'm an incompetent bloody idiot who's started so high I've left myself
nowhere vocally to go!!'

Head in hand, he collapses on the stage management's table and blubs. He
emerges weeping with laughter.

(These bouts of self-criticism are wonderfully diverting. He splinters the tensions
of these highly concentrated rehearsals with so many laughs.)

MH (pacing the floor): Rethink . . . rethink . . . the man's a Catholic. He's about
to commit a fearful sin. I must be appalled when I realise I'm on the brink of suicide
. . . the enormity of what he's doing slowly dawns on him. Must get his *reason*
working again . . . from this point Pinfold wins—he's got a grip on his reason again,
that's why . . . once he's got a grip on his reason . . .

This gives him a lower vocal note to start from.

And it carries him through to the climax of his defeat of the demons with his
reading of *Westward Ho?*.

In his novel Waugh uses no direct quotes from Kingsley. The whole passage is
singularly low-key. All over in a couple of paragraphs.

In Harwood's play it covers two foolscap pages. Contains a great virtuoso *tour
de force* in an ensemble for eleven voices.

His choice from Kingsley's text is brilliant, descending into babble about Goths and
Visigoths when Pinfold senses he's got his enemies on the run. He ends on a
crescendo of gibberish, with the fleeing Furies screaming 'Leave the bloody ship!'

I find that last line wickedly funny. I rumble it as Harwood's device to get us
all off the stage and out into that great echoing Royal Exchange concourse. So that
the reverberating howls of banishment diminish into nothingness as the demons
vanish from Pinfold's mind . . .

It's one of the few flourishes which Harwood has invented outside the text of
Waugh's own dialogue.

Precisely how to act 'reading' all this boring stuff is a 'quondarum' for MH.

He tries reading-acting in various ways.

If he gives the text sense it might not sound boring enough. Or if he colours it with
any expression . . .

He varies the pace and the volume. Then he tries sense into nonsense . . .

Then he tries reading it straight ('and if that wasn't boring enough for you, I don't
know what is.' Thank you, Mr Hordern, we'll let you know. Don't call us, etc.)

He settles for a lucid but saw-like drone. To begin with. Then as Elliott brings in the interjections of Pinfold's tormentors, and as the tempo gets faster and faster, MH hammers the words with the force of a pile-driver.

Relentless, relentless . . .

The scene works up to a cracking climax. I've never heard a monotone used with such virtuosity before.

As we all rush off, we all shout spontaneously, 'Please, Mr Hordern, leave the bloody *stage!*'

FRIDAY, 2 SEPTEMBER REHEARSAL ROOM
ACT I: LYCHPOLE SCENES

After the high-strikes of rehearsing Act Two for two days, these scenes seem as tranquil as Gloucestershire itself. The lines seem to have stayed where they were—glued in at the last rehearsal. The makeshift props have become old friends. Dangerous that.
Makeshifts take on a veracity of their own. So when we do get the actual bits and pieces at the dress rehearsal, we shall have to unlearn and relearn them.
And there are still the theatre's own performers to be added—its enormous battery of electronics.

Over the teacups, MH says that *Jumpers* and *Lear* were longer parts and that *Jumpers* was more exhausting to play than *Lear*. He's hoping that *Pinfold* will emancipate him from the millstone that *Jumpers* has become.

I ponder the ratio of lines spoken by MH to his reactions to lines spoken by the rest of us. Can't do the maths but it must be even-stevens at least . . .

Pinfold: Did I tell you about the wash-hand stand?
MH: That line worries me. Obviously he didn't otherwise he wouldn't be telling him now.

It's chewing-the-bone time. Gnawing, spitting out, adding, subtracting. Is there something we've missed . . .

Elliott points out that Pinfold's previous line is 'my memory is playing me tricks'. And we all do it. We start to tell a story, realise we've already told the listener, but it doesn't stop us.
MH dubious.

How heavily drugged is Pinfold in these opening scenes?
He never stops taking pills, medicines, sleeping draughts.
Elliott: Very heavily. But don't *you* do it. We'll do it.

Elliott works on the principle of 'Let him who plays the King just *be*'. So long as everybody else treats him like a king, the audience will accept him as one. He asks Peggy (Mrs Pinfold) to have difficulty getting through to Pinfold when she's talking to him.
'Remember—her line is "You're doped, darling, up to the eyes."'

With this perfect piece of directing, the action suddenly leaps forward.
MH: Should Pinfold apologise to his wife for not taking her on the cruise?
Elliott: No. What you were doing was lovely. Don't gild it. Leave it as it was.

An endorsement like that is as comforting as a hug.

End of the third week of rehearsals.

FOURTH WEEK
MONDAY, 5 SEPTEMBER

I met MH in the car park this morning. On our way to the theatre we talked about the play (what else). I told him that I admired what he was doing with Pinfold. He said, 'Dear old friend, are you sure you're not investing this performance with what you've known of all the previous parts I've played?'

Am I?

I don't think so. I get the feeling that his search for Pinfold is being enjoyed as much by the rest of the company as by me.

A.M.

This morning the lines which have been selected by Elliott for pre-recording are to be taped.

The actors troop down into one of the Royal Exchange Building's vast ventilator shafts. The accoustics for sound recording are perfect there.

Is there any part of this remarkable building which cannot be put to practical use? The whole place is like some gigantic theatrical toybox.

P.M.:
REHEARSAL ROOM

A word rehearsal.

The text is prattled by us all in a relaxed, discursive tone. This, curiously, reveals the narrative very clearly. MH also talks his way through his moves, business, change of costume, change of clothes. (His one exit from the arena, before Pinfold goes on board the *Caliban*, is to put on hat, coat and muffler.)

The crocodile rivers are charted—here be pitfalls, plotfalls and pratfalls. We make mental timings of our quick changes and the lack of time we'll have to make them in.

There are some awful gaps to be plugged . . .

TUESDAY, 6 SEPTEMBER
A.M.: BACK IN THE THEATRE

Air, space, and—now that the production is coming together—more and more new faces, the technicians.

ACT II:
CABIN SCENE

The cabin set is wheeled on, almost finished. The copper pipes which nearly cleaved MH's head are painted cream, having been welded into position.

The first of Pinfold's voices is that of the preaching clergyman.

MH is unsure how to time his reaction to it.

Elliott suggests it should come after MH has sat on the bunk. The comicality of MH's astonishment is trebled.

By the end of this Denunciation-of-Billy scene, MH has changed into his dinner suit—now timed so that he puts his shoes on as the hymn ends.

Elliott wonders whether the clergyman would cause Pinfold to be rather more anxious than MH has been playing it. 'Yes.'

Pinfold (to Glover): 'Nice to *see* you again.'
This line gives trouble.
Why does Pinfold suddenly interrupt his own totally self- absorbed thoughts to be affable to a fellow-passenger? c.f. ACT ONE PINFOLD: 'Why does everyone except me find it so easy to be nice?'

There seems to be no reason for Pinfold to 'be nice'.

Elliott changes the entrance door from which Glover approaches Pinfold. He is now surprised by Glover, rather than seeing him before his mutterings are interrupted. 'Does that make it easier? Try it.'
It doesn't.

This line is not a mere social gambit. The line 'Nice to see you again' is a condensation of elapsed time. In the novel, Pinfold assumes that the lapse of time since their previous meeting has been far longer than it actually was.

c.f. ACT II. Captain: 'This is only our fifth day out you know.'
Pinfold: (perplexed) Are you sure . . . It seems much longer.'

MH tries a different reading: 'Nice to see you again.' (After all this time—that awful prayer meeting last night: understood.)

In this play of reactions, as usual Glover's reaction is the clue. MH tries the line accusingly, as if Glover has been deliberately avoiding Pinfold over several days. MH grunts and says gruffly, 'Huh! Nice to see *you* again.' Glover looks startled. That seems to work.

Another block removed. This one takes twenty minutes to sort out. Back and back again.
Elliott: How would it be if the cabin set was moved round? A change in its position would denote lapse of time, distance travelled by the ship . . . Try it.

Fosker and the Young Man turn it during the Undergraduate Taunting scene. They trundle the bewildered Pinfold round and round. It adds horrible menace to the action—very frightening for poor old Pinfold . . .
Just as Ian Hastings and Jeffrey Perry (Young Man) are spinning the set, one of its castors falls loose. The cabin sits broken-winged. Consternation! It's like a street accident. Help is summoned from the Workshop across the hall, carpenters with their tools, ambulance men, to give it first aid. The whole building seethes with denizens who are never far away.
Blacksmiths, wheelwrights, cooks, jesters, jongleurs, lords . . . it's all a bit like being in a mediaeval castle.

Becher's Brook. (Second stab at it.) Despair.
MH: I am not the same man that I've been playing for the last three-quarters of an hour. Why do I suddenly say this very amusing but inconsequential speech? And may I please have the props next time. And every time.

He tries the speech again and again because he must solve it . . . But eventually we leave it, unresolved. It's the only remaining part of the play now where one feels that MH is unnerved.

We move on to the next cabin scene. Pinfold is reading a book. MH picks up the prop book and starts to read. It's a 'make-shift', a book of party games. He's opened it at suggestions for an imagined game of consequences. The infantile example reduces him to giggles and he reads some of the dafter lines aloud to us. After his wretchedness at having fallen yet again at Becher's, this is as good a way as any to let off steam. It works like a charm.

p.m.: BACK IN THE REHEARSAL ROOM

Elliott took notes this morning. So we work through these carefully. Going back over and over the scenes.

This morning the size of the theatre with its attendants, air and space, seemed to diminish the performances. This afternoon, the rehearsal room appears to enhance them. Is there a danger that up here we are flattered into thinking that the work is better than it will be when we take it downstairs again?

(I can remember the time when I thought that acting was easy.)

It's been a long day. Full of having to adjust to circumstances. By the end of it our heads are full of our own 'notes' to ourselves as well.

Then having to meet the journalists. Why is it always so deeply depressing? Why do they always appear to lack any kind of vitality, wit or humour? Why haven't they done their homework? And why do they ask such dispiriting questions?

We sat in two formal rows on the seven-seater benches, facing each other. Actors v Journalists.
To MH: How do you feel, knowing that Alec Guinness was asked to play the part first?
MH: Do you know, it happens so often in the profession I never really mind who's been asked to play a part like this before me so long as I'm the one who eventually plays it.
To MH: Have you ever had a nervous breakdown yourself?
MH (selecting, presumably at random, one of them in particular): Oh, I think we're all pretty near it most of the time. Don't you?

Etc, etc.

It is 5.30 p.m.
MH: May we go back on what we've done so far this afternoon to see what's gone in? Just for the links and the changes we've made? Not with acting. I don't think I could do any more acting today.

It is 7.15 p.m.

As he and I leave the theatre tonight MH says he feels that the play hasn't progressed at all. Things that were funny at the first reading have ceased to be funny . . . details were obfuscating the line . . .

It is the nadir.

Today is The Day.

WEDNESDAY, 7 SEPTEMBER
A.M.: FIRST RUN-THROUGH OF THE PLAY IN THE THEATRE.

We have lights, and for the first time there is feeling that there is a performance afoot. No sound effects. Diana is still reading them aloud. But lights.

ACT ONE: LYCHPOLE

MH now has rubber tips on his walking sticks. The floor of the stage is polished parquet and until now it has been difficult for him to lean on them properly without fear of falling.

Angel enters, bears down on Pinfold. MH leans back on his sticks in an attitude of complete repugnance for his visitor. The walking sticks suspend him, spider-like, (reflecting the angle at which the theatre building itself is hung in suspension).

MH remains imperiously spread for the next few speeches.

   . . . wonder why the rehearsal now feels sluggish, off-key . . .

Clergyman/Billy scene.

The blackthorn walking stick suddenly tears MH's hand and he needs (mild) first aid. He goes off somewhere in the building and we all sit in subdued silence. There are splashes of blood on the Cabin Set floor.

With all the doors closed, the auditorium becomes a sort of capsule – the noise and bustle of the rest of the building going on outside the cocoon. It's a slightly eerie feeling . . .

MH comes back. He lifts his performance. Adrenalin?

Becher's Brook.

Today there is hot soup, rolls, champagne, cutlery, crockery . . . The fence is taken impeccably. Up, over and on.

A bit of telepathy between MH and Elliott:

Halfway through Pinfold's 'I am alone' speech, MH suddenly announces: 'I've gone off the boil.' He asks if he has the right feeling, pacing up and down the cabin like this.

Elliott: Well, you're changing your clothes at this point, aren't you?

MH (sits):   Ah!

They look at each other.

ME says he's been thinking about these constant changes of clothes. He has spoken to Stephen Doncaster, and thinks that it will be better for the play as well as making life more comfortable for the audience and the actor, if MH makes no costume changes at all.

Not at all?

No. Remain in one suit for the entire play.

If MH agrees, that is.

MH agrees.

Oh, boy, does he agree!

Later . . .

Elliott: Make more of the 'garlanded hero'.

      MH cheekily tucks his hand into his jacket, Nelson-style.

p.m.: BACK IN THE REHEARSAL ROOM

Notes on this morning's run in the theatre.

The Adagio (the Love Scene).

It's now too slow. The pauses which seemed to be unspoken eloquence in the rehearsal room yesterday disintegrated into turgid sentiment in the theatre today.

Then MH has to go off to the sick bay again. A metal splinter this time.

Another interruption. For the stills photographer. We pose in groups of four in one of the large dressing rooms, staring straight at the camera.

These photographs are for the programme. (Eek!)

THURSDAY, 8 SEPTEMBER

a.m.: Run-through of entire play in the theatre.

p.m.: Take the morning's work to pieces up in the rehearsal room.

Ronald Harwood has rejoined us.

Bechers Brook defeats MH. RH asks if there is any help *he* can offer. MH shakes bloodhound chops at him. How can RH suggest any other help than cutting the damned speech altogether.?

RH: Let's cut the speech.

MH (stung): No, by God, we won't cut the speech! I'll say it if it kills me.

Ah well!

Pinfold's tormentors take the forms of Duty Officers reciting a log which graphs the degrees of his insanity. They hurl factory noises at him, to test him while he's trying to sleep. Ten of us. Plus sound effects. The dialogue for this scene is rapid-fire one-line observations to be delivered from points all around the first gallery.

Since the lines are to be spoken in disembodied monotones, the actors can't cling to any quirks of characterisation which might help them to memorise the lines. It takes forty-five minutes to rehearse the single page of dialogue.

Just as we get the rattle-pace going, one of us trips and the rhythm is thrown. Memories become embarrassing blanks. Again and again.

MH, although lying on the bunk acting being asleep, has to react to each line, since at the end of the fireworks he has to leap out of bed, turn on the light and rage powerfully enough to stop the towering din of amplified machinery. So we'd better get it right.

Begin again.

I think its one of the most nerve-wracking things I've had to do. The jitters are infectious. We all apologise profusely when it's our turn to stumble.

When hysteria begins to set in—Elliott (quietly): Let's leave it. Cup of tea.

We all collapse, frayed.

Considering that it's the only piece of sustained tension the rest of us have had to maintain all day, we ought to be ashamed of our lack of stamina, I suppose. Especially as MH goes from aria to aria and is still talking his way through. And never remaining still for longer than thirty seconds at a time. But then, it's always easier to dictate one's own pace than to be hassled.

This play needs practice as well as rehearsal.

FRIDAY, 9 SEPTEMBER
A.M.: RUN-THROUGH IN THE THEATRE

Before each of these runs-through in the theatre, MH sets up his own private notes. Chris Monks sits with MH's script and, during the action at a nod from MH, Chris marks the script 'for further study'.

After working with this talk-through method for nearly a month now, it fazes none of us when he peppers the dialogue with '*that* speech'.

Today and Saturday are the final rehearsals with just the text, the actors, the stage management, the director and the playwright.
After these two days—the deluge.

P.M. REHEARSAL ROOM
ACT 1: LYCHPOLE, THE OPENING SPEECH OF THE PLAY.

Pinfold: 'The Ordeal of Gilbert Pinfold. A conversation piece. Chapter One. Portrait of the Artist in Middle-age,' . . . etc.

Harwood: Any author reading his own words tends to read them as *well* as possible. Pinfold's proud of his creation and he enjoys this first paragraph.

MH: Not too much emphasis though. Don't you think otherwise it becomes an actor reading?

Elliott: 'At the time of his adventure. . .' is actually a most pleasurable recollection. The horror is recollected later. 'Was it then that the other events occurred? They seemed trivial at the time.' . . . that's the clue, I think. 'They seemed trivial at the time, but later . . . grew to importance' . . . That's when the horror of it strikes him. Later.

MH: Ah!

There's marrow yet to be drawn out of the bone . . .

Elliott: (Turns to the rest of us) Anyone not on until the first ship scene won't be needed for at least forty-five minutes. Do go down to the Green Room or wherever.

As usual, none of us leaves.
We've become compulsive viewers.

The wash-hand stand speech.

MH confesses to RH that he has deliberately replaced the word 'trophy' because to MH trophy represents an animal's head, a cup . . .

MH: I know its Waugh's word but it gives me a mental hiccup.

RH defends trophy.

RH: Surely a trophy implies something which has been won. The burden of the speech being that Waugh, like Queen Mary, admired some possession of a friend and hoped to be given it. It was then placed on a mental plinth. Hence Waugh's immaculate choice of the word.

MH had substituted 'object', which he acknowledges to be totally inadequate, but . . . He also acknowledges that not only is it inadequate—it doesn't work.
He grins and concedes. Just testing.

Actually that's the only deviation from the authorised version that he's made. Apart from small adhesive words that bind the cuts together. And his formidable battery of snorts, oohs, ahs, grunts, whistles, moans and groans.

He goes back over the speech. 'Trophy' settles back into the warp.

After Drake's exit, Pinfold left alone goes back to his pills and potions for the umpteenth time. Having taken another dose, he rings Telegrams.

Elliott: Lift the phone and say 'telegrams' *then* pour the medicine. That'll keep it alive while you're waiting for them to answer.

Pinfold: 'We await your further instructions . . .,'
            etc.

MH: Travel brochures to be set discovered open, envelopes without flaps, please. Spectacles still on desk. Remember at this point to put glasses into pocket after examining brochures . . .

He's still talking his way through every bit of business. Chris Monks faithfully marks up the study script.

Pinfold: '. . . kindly investigate wanton inefficiency your office. Pinfold.'

Pinfold's anger trips MH. He slithers into breathless incoherence and ends on his verbal backside.

MH: Sorry. Rushing the lines. Go back.

Goes back. This time he allows Pinfold's anger to rumble. Firm, unhurried. It becomes Churchillian.

Got it.

MH: Aha! Waughish not waspish!

Nods to Chris Monks, who makes a note. 'Waughish not waspish?'

During these opening Lychpole scenes, MH has to pour drink and swallow pills no less than ten separate times. Marrying his enormously long speeches with the complexities of all these bits of business has taken an infinite amount of patient practising. Having succeeded in making it all completely unobtrusive—can he now make it work for him?

Pinfold: 'I must take foolscap paper' . . . etc During this speech, Pinfold takes yet another swig. How would it be if Mrs Pinfold gives him a look and he takes this not surreptitiously as before, but almost as a toast. To his coming voyage!

It would be a welcome variation!

Try it.

Keep it in.

It adds a jaunty air of anticipation for the next scene—aboard

SS *Caliban*.

ACT II
FIRST CABIN SCENE

MH will not now change his clothes. So there is no need for the suitcase to be unpacked. Ron Emslie, having studied how to unpack like a professional steward, has only to take out Pinfold's dressing gown and sponge-bag.

MH says 'I'll unpack later', Ron stows the bag and exits. Isn't that the story of an actor's life? He mugs up a skill so that he can perform it well enough to convince any adepts who may be in the audience, and then it ends up on the cutting room floor.

FIRST SALOON SCENE

Pinfold's first meeting with his fellow passengers. Gareth Forwood (Glover) decides to give MH a clout of hearty camaraderie. This reduces MH to giggles. When they go back on it, MH pinches up his face into Pinfold's disdain at being clouted. This reduces Gareth to giggles.

CABIN SCENE: CLERGYMAN/BILLY SCENE

There is a real hairbrush in the sponge-bag! MH seizes it with cries of joy. He can now time brushing his hair with his reactions to the lascivious lines that Pinfold thinks he hears.

DINING SALOON

A tight six around the Captain's table.

Elliott warns us that the table will come in on a truck, on a rostrum six inches from the floor. The stewards (Emslie and Branche) will have to stand on the rostrum to serve the champagne and the soup.
A very tight *eight*.

So tight that, in order to give Branche (Black Steward) room to mop up the spilled champagne, MH lifts his elbows in the air, hands above his head.

He decides to leave them there and plays the next few lines with them aloft. He then becomes foolishly aware of them and lowers them—Pinfold discomfited.

This new bit of business tickles MH enormously. He laughs uproariously.
MH: Sometimes one's best inventions come when one is most tired!

But the next page is Becher's. And he falls. Neck and crop.

He puts his head in his hands again. And blubs and blubs and blubs.

Oh, dear, tears before bedtime. When, just a few minutes before, things had been going so wonderfully well.

But his actor's misery is real. He *cannot* find a sequence of thought to lead him into this speech. Yet he simply must.

ME insists that he repeats and repeats and repeats it. MH protests that this will waste everybody else's time.
ME: On the contrary, [gently] That's why we're all here.

MH takes the speech in isolation five times. First just for the words, without acting. Then as he grows more confident he eases Pinfold into the speech. Then he goes back to a few of the previous lines.
Then we go back over the whole scene . . .

Two-cups-of-tea

CABIN SCENE. Voice over: Captain and Goneril's voices are discussing the torture.
ME: This scene consists entirely of Pinfold's reaction shots. Let's take it from the top.
CAPTAIN: (Trumpet solo) I want you to know that a quantity of valuable metal was sacrificed last night for the welfare of a single seaman . . . (etc).

Elliott's hands fan wide and flat, moving outwards in an even line, riding gently—conducting . . .

Elliott: There's nothing alarming to Pinfold in the Captain's speech. He entirely approves of what the Captain is saying . . .

MH grunts and nods Pinfold's approval over the speech.

Elliott: It's Goneril's voice that brings him up sharp.

MH does some what-am-I-hearing acting.

ME points, Bobbyrolli-like, to the trombone of Willo and Harry LW (generals). They follow his beat and whoop their lines.

Elliott: The generals' voices *suddenly* cheer him up.

MH seizes it and leaps up.

Elliott: Good. Good. Something to do. He knows how to handle military men. Now he's full of purpose. Splendid.

MH: Well, it may not be quite right yet, but it makes the scene a good deal livelier . . . instead of my just sitting glumly in the cabin. Ah, but then he loses confidence again, doesn't he? Won't that drop the scene on the floor again?

ME: That's all right. We've had a nice change of tempo. And immediately after that short lapse into mental disturbance, it's morning. Light change. You come out of your cabin. Young people come on. Deck games. Other passengers enter. Everything normal. And we're off again. Into the next scene.

Off and into an incoherent muddle.
The 'next scene' is on the deck outside Pinfold's cabin, and in the saloon. Using the entire perimeter of the stage.

As passengers and crew, ten of us enter. The Young People play deck games, around one half of the stage—merry-laughing acting.
The older bodies make their ways around to the other side of the stage and into the saloon 'set'—having-drinks acting. During Pinfold's probing dialogue with Glover and then with the Captain, we should all be noting with discomfited surprise, Pinfold's eccentric appearance and odd behaviour: concerted number.

The trouble is that so far this scene hasn't been properly orchestrated.
We are all acting and reacting independently.
We're all doing our own thing all over the arena. and the result is a bag of manure. The scene has no focus.

It collapses into complete shambles when the medicine ball flies across the stage, bounces playfully off MH's head and starts giving its own performance.

ME calms us all down and we all sit down and say the lines to numbers. While we're doing this, he talks MH through his moves. He then asks us to repeat it, when he adds the tempo. He then slams the climax of the scene into position and isolates it:

Mrs S: Tight as a tick.

Elliott: Pinfold overhears that on the move back to his cabin. Turns. Hold his disbelief.

Captain: Are you sure?

Mr S: Simply plastered.

Elliott: Pinfold turns from them disdainfully. Pauses. Then turns back to his cabin. The deck passengers and the Captain, make your exits after Michael's final turn into his cabin. But not before. Try it.

We try it. Back and back again and again. Until we all know precisely what we're doing. And why.

Undisciplined ensemble-playing looks sloppy enough behind a proscenium arch, goodness knows. In the round, it is a total disaster.

SATURDAY, 10 SEPTEMBER
THE THEATRE

Our final chance of rehearsing in the theatre alone, without the technicians. Next week, dress rehearsals and the full *batterie de jeu*.

When we arrive this morning, the stage is already set with the actual Lychpole furniture. A handsome mahogany leather-topped desk and a beautiful swivel-chair. Ian Hastings as BBC technician has to push Pinfold forwards towards his desk while he is actually sitting in his chair—MH is already on his knees examining the castors on the chair!

There are also as many of the actual hand props that the stage management has been able to muster. (Someone should take photographs of an actor the first time he is given the actual props. We behave like children at Christmas, when the bus tickets and empty shoe-boxes have suddenly turned into 'real things'.)

ACT I:
LYCHPOLE
Pinfold: . . . I have known periods of literary composition when I would find the sentences I had written during the day running in my head, the words shifting and changing colour kaleidoscopically, so that I would again and again climb out of bed, pad down to the library, make a minute correction, return to my room, lie in the dark dazzled by the pattern of vocables until obliged once more to descend to the manuscript.

Not a bad description of this morning's work.

MH: Stop the watch. Do I at this point take the ever-larger and larger doses of sleeping draught in brandy or crème de menthe?
Elliott: Crème de menthe.

Dazzled by the colour of the actual props. . .

MH goes on making his own 'minute corrections' over and over again. Chris Monks still taking the nod. Marking the passages.

After the run-through, we have notes. Elliott's notes. Harwood's notes. MH's notes (via Chris).

First ME talks MH through his reactions to the Voice-Over demons. So that when the technology hits him next week, MH will be quite confident that he knows what he is doing.

Then we rehearse the notes:
Undergraduate Scene.
Tilly has been singing 'Gilbert the Filbert' outside the porthole of the cabin.

Actually onstage.

MH: But I've been acting that I hear her voice coming from somewhere else. From up there [pointing to the speakers]. How would it be if, after she's finished the song, I open to look for her and find nobody. If she dodged away. Wouldn't that point the cruelty of their teasing? It would certainly make me feel more isolated.

Tilly moves away. The Young Men circle the cabin.

Elliott: The Young Men will be more menacing to Pinfold if they are quieter when they are speaking to each other. Only raising their voices when they are addressing and taunting Pinfold.

Same scene.

Fosker: He's locked the door.

Pinfold: I haven't.

Elliott: Try making 'I haven't' more spontaneously surprised. Rather than defiant.

The blackthorn stick. The actual one at last. MH clings to it throughout Act One. Does he need it during Act II when he says he feels better? No. Discard it after Act I.

But he does take it up at one point. After the Under-graduates' taunting. He seizes it in order to thrash them and to protect himself. Consequently he has a lot of fun with it during the following scene, when he's searching for the hidden present.

ACT II
The Dining Saloon. Breakfast Scene.

When the tablelamp emits the hooligans' voices, MH has rehearsed the scene sitting left of tablelamp. Elliot changes his position to right of tablelamp. His flabbergasted reaction can now be seen by a far larger section of the house.

Saloon. Scene following Captain's inserted speech 'Extra man on board . . .'. (Murdoch) By changing MH's position to the outer of the four identical saloon chairs, Elliott has caused him to have to lean and look upwards at Ken Randle (Murdoch).

Pinfold leers knowingly at Murdoch, who finds this behaviour even more alarming than Pinfold's previous staring. MH has been playing this scene introspectively. Assuming that Pinfold imagines that the importance and the burden of the Captain's message was for his ears alone.

By including Murdoch into the conspiracy like this, it opens out the comedy. And also the ludicrousness of Pinfold's trauma as it appears to the other passengers, through Murdoch's reaction to it.

TEMPTATION SCENE

Towards the end of this morning's rehearsal, I was standing in one of the theatre's aisles watching this scene (when Goneril is goading Pinfold into taking his own life). 'Go on, Gilbert. Jump. In you go.'

Harwood was sitting on one of the steps in the aisle, also watching.

Until now MH has rehearsed the scene with Pinfold standing at the ship's rail contemplating the sea below. The man has been driven to the end of his tether, finally tormented to it by the unbearable clamour of amplified factory machinery.

Today is the first time MH has had the actual rail. He suddenly stops. He tests the rail and then asks to try the suicide attempt in a different way.
MH: As it is at the moment, it's more reminiscent of Jeffrey's vomiting over the side than of a chap about to sling himself overboard.

MH goes back into his cabin. Lies down on the bunk. 'Go on, Gilbert. Jump. In you go.'

Suddenly, to everybody's amazement, MH comes catapulting out of the cabin and hurls himself into the air. He lands on top of the rail, balancing on his right foot, steadying himself with his left hand. For a moment he hovers like a gymnast. There is a gasp as he totters . . . Then a sigh of relief when he leaps back on to the stage.

I'm not sure whether the gasps were in admiration of his agility or whether we thought that he was going to end up in the one-and-nines. But as a *coup de théâtre*, it is a stunner.

Back again.
It wasn't a fluke.
Back and back again until he gets it exactly right.

Harwood is grinning.
He actually says, 'He's got it!'.

When I was last in Manchester, I watched Orwain Arwel Hughes conduct the Hallé Orchestra and Chorus in a gala performance of Belshazzar's Feast, in celebration of Walton's seventieth birthday.
It was one of the most exciting things I've ever seen. From the moment that Hughes raised his baton, he lifted himself up on his toes and literally stayed there throughout the performance. He danced his performers through the piece.

I feel the same way about Hordern's Pinfold.

That funny old stumblebum dances his way through the entire play.

Gwen Cherrell, © 1993

Gilbert Pinfold sees it Through! A review which appeared in the *Sunday Times*, 18 September 1977 of *The Ordeal of Gilbert Pinfold*.

Bernard Levin

With a last sad look at my bucket and spade, I return, blinking at the unaccustomed darkness, to a week's theatrical fishing that has landed mostly tiddlers. Mostly, but oh! not entirely, for there is a very Behemoth to be seen at the Royal Exchange, Manchester, in Michael Hordern's performance as the haunted hero of *The Ordeal of Gilbert Pinfold*.

Adapted by Ronald Harwood from Evelyn Waugh's autobiographical shipboard novel recounting the progress of a severe breakdown into paranoiac hallucinations, the play works uncommonly well, walking the book's line between absurdity and terror as Pinfold's accusing voices multiply, and his imaginary tormentors grow more vicious and more cruel. (The elaborate sound effects, without which the thing could hardly be done at all, are the flawless work of Tim Foster and George Glossop.)

The play is strong, spare and lucid (though Mr Harwood's task was presumably lightened by the fact that much of the original consists of dialogue, and all of it of Waugh's diamond prose); it rightly sounds a final note of hope and triumph ('I have endured a great ordeal, and emerged the victor—unaided'). Also Michael Elliott's direction most plausibly suggests the swirling horror in Pinfold's mind, as the figmentary persecutors fill the open space around the cage of the victim's cabin; and there is a lovely girlish performance by Lindsay Duncan as the innocent among the villains. But Mr Hordern's the thing.

And what a thing! He is off the stage for no more than a few seconds in the play's 150 minutes, and this performance is surely the crown of an immensely distinguished career. To start with, what other actor could so shamble and groan and grimace like this, without ever hinting at exaggeration, let alone self-aggrandisement? (Only Guinness.) What other performer could so suggest a man fighting to keep from his consciousness the conviction that he is mad? (Only Scofield.) How many others could simultaneously—simultaneously not alternately—have us shaking with laughter and transfixed with pity? (Only Olivier.) Who else combines such classical diction with such expressive intonation? (Only Gielgud.) Who can match this generosity of gesture (just watch the florid brow-mopping if you want to see how a great actor creates from a common action a meticulously controlled theatrical effect) to this care in timing and movement? Only Hordern, I think, who with this performance has made himself the peer of that illustrious company.

As I left, the celebrated echo of the Royal Exchange was adding to the cheers. They needed no addition; they deserved multiplication.

ACKNOWLEDGEMENTS

The author and publisher are grateful to *The Times* for permission to reproduce the photographs of Sir Michael Hordern fishing on the Lambourn by Nick Rogers, on the back of the jacket and inside the book.

They are also grateful to Zoe Dominic for permission to reproduce her photographs of Sir Michael Hordern as Anthony Absolute in the National Theatre production of *The Rivals* on the back of the jacket and inside the book and Sir Michael Hordern and Julie Covington in *Jumpers*, also at the National Theatre.

They are also grateful to the Estate of Angus McBean for permission to reproduce the photographs of Sir Michael Hordern and Beatrix Lehmann in *Macbeth* at the Old Vic, Flora Robson and Sir Michael Hordern in *Ghosts* and Sir Michael Hordern as Caliban in *The Tempest*.

They are also grateful to Clive Francis for permission to reproduce on page ii his caricature '© Clive Francis' of the author in the role of Sir Anthony Absolute in *The Rivals*.

Index